ALUN RICHARDS was born in Pontypridd in 1929 and, apart from service in the Royal Navy, has lived in South Wales for most of his life. His novels include *The Home Patch, Home to an Empty House* and *Ennal's Point*. He is also the author of several volumes of short stories, *Dai Country* (which received the Welsh Arts Council's literary prize), *The Former Miss Merthyr Tydfil*, and *Selected Stories*. He is the Editor of the *Penguin Book of Welsh Short Stories* and two volumes of *Penguin Sea Stories*. He has written extensively for radio and television, including frequent contributions to such popular TV series as *The Onedin Line*.

Alun Richards has also written about rugby. He scripted the BBC Film *A Touch of Glory* which celebrated the centenary of the Welsh Rugby Union and is the author of a companion pictorial volume. Most recently, he has adapted a novel offering a solution to the mystery of the *Mary Celeste* for Radio 4 and scripted documentary films dealing with aspects of the lives of persons as varied as Luciano Pavarotti and the Lions centre, Scott Gibbs.

He has also lectured for the Department of Adult Education at the University College of Swansea which awarded him an Honorary Fellowship in 1985 and he has recently received an Honorary Doctorate from the University of Glamorgan.

Also by Alun Richards:

Novels
The Elephant You Gave Me
The Home Patch
A Woman of Experience
Home to an Empty House
Ennal's Point
Barque Whisper

Short Story Collections
Dai Country
The Former Miss Merthyr Tydfil

History
A Touch of Glory (100 Years of Welsh Rugby)

As Editor
The Penguin Book of Welsh Short Stories
The Penguin Book of Sea Stories
Against the Waves (Sea Stories)

Plays
The Big Breaker
The Victuallers' Ball
The Snowdropper
The Horizontal life

Television Plays
Going Like a Fox
O Captain, My Captain
Nothing to Pay
Hear the Tiger, See the Bay
The Hot Potato Boys
Ready for the Glory
Taffy Came to My House
Who Steals My Name
Albinos in Black
The Straight and Narrow
The Princely Gift
Harry Lifters

Television Adaptations
The Schoolmaster (Simenon)
Vessel of Wrath (W. Somerset Maugham)
Love and Mr Lewisham (H. G. Wells)
Acting Captain (Alun Lewis)

Television Series
Ennal's Point

Carwyn

A
Personal
Memoir

Alun Richards

CHRISTOPHER DAVIES
~ SWANSEA 2002 ~

First published in Great Britain by Michael Joseph Ltd.
44 Bedford Square, London WC1 in1984

Re-published in 2002 by
Christopher Davies (Publishers) Ltd.
P.O. Box 403, Swansea, SA1 4YF

A CIP catalogue record for this book is
available from the British Library.

ISBN 0 7154 0741 4

Printed and bound in Wales by
Dinefwr Press Ltd.
Rawlings Road, Llandybie
Carmarthenshire, SA18 3YD

This book is for another four
of Carwyn's friends

Stephen
Michael
Jessica
and
Daniel

Contents

List of Illustrations
(Between pages 82 & 83)

Acknowledgements

My thanks are due to the family and friends of Carwyn James, in particular his brother, Dewi, and his sister, Gwen, for access to his papers and permission to reprint family photographs; to BBC Wales for permission to consult archive material, and to the many people who spared me their time and talked to me at length. I would also like to express my thanks to the editors of the *Guardian* and the *Western Mail* for permission to quote from articles written by Carwyn. I have also quoted from the work of Gwenallt and T. H. Parry Williams in translation, from *The Barry John Story*, John Taylor's *The Decade of the Dragon*, the *History of Gwendraeth Grammar School*, *The History of Llandovery College*, an article by Dr Hywel Francis of the South Wales Miners' Library, 'The Anthracite Strike and Disturbances of 1925', printed in *Llafur*, the journal of Welsh historical studies, and from recorded reminiscences of Dai Dan Evans, former General Secretary of the South Wales Miners, reprinted in the *South Wales Evening Post*. My thanks are due to the authors, translators and publishers, and also to the librarians of the Oystermouth branch of the West Glamorgan County Library.

Introduction

The moment was ordinary and of the kind which is habitual in every house these days. Enveloped in a cosy armchair of a Sunday evening, lounging deep into its comfort, leaning back, his forearm at right angles with the arm rest and wielding the. eternal untipped cigarette between his fingers, Carwyn James watched television.

He was earnestly transfixed by a wildlife programme. This seemed odd. I could easily imagine him rapt by a political narrative, a programme dealing with some obscure corner of the arts, or a profile or retrospective of an unsung hero of sport. These after all were aspects of his own interests which had evolved to form his personality and which he permitted the world to recognise and to acknowledge. He had stood as Plaid Cymru candidate in Llanelli, had lectured on Welsh literature; and of Chekov he knew a great deal. His rugby exploits were, of course, legendary. There were many sides to Carwyn James.

The interest in natural history, however, seemed fugitive and random. He was a denizen more suited to parlours and drawing rooms not a backpacker among the beetles of the marshes or viewing the snouting habits of warthogs in inhospitable forests. If he needed to be outdoors he would do so in a tracksuit suggesting ideas to his players, whether in Llandovery College or Llanelli and other less familiar corners of the world, on how better to use a rugby ball. Otherwise he would be found in a lounge suit with a gin and tonic on order.

"Television is a wonderful invention," he said, without turning, speaking as if to himself or to the screen in front of him. "It makes things which are strange seem familiar and brings what is foreign into your home. Trouble is everything is made to seem so commonplace. We take everything for granted so that we are in danger of losing our sense of wonder."

It was, if anything, that sense of wonder which he brought with him to rugby football and which he tried to transmit, and invariably succeeded, to those players who played under him in Stradey Park, Rovigo and, most famously and tellingly of all, the Lions on their unforgettable tour to New Zealand in 1971. Time, as we all understand, lends enchantment to the dream and to look back on those days is to invest in them an aura which has the magic of innocence; bold and perfectly playful.

In the thirty-one years that have passed since the Lions' unique success and almost twenty years since Carwyn died in Amsterdam so much seems to have changed in rugby union. If the manner of play has been transformed – more body collision, fewer ghostly evasions, and the reasons why a man chooses to play rugby – for money and not necessarily for recreation or for the simple honour, so has our mood and vision of glory shifted, too.

These are melancholy days for Welsh rugby. Only one Championship title since 1979 (shared with France in 1988), similarly for the Triple Crown (same year). There has been no Grand Slam since 1978. It has been a bleak time. There is no sign of the sun ever glinting from behind the dark and deepening clouds; no flinting spark of Wales's genius for rugby football to give life to the hope that one day it will be as good again and as we of a certain generation once knew it.

At times such as these, Carwyn is ever-present at the wake. We wonder what he might have made of it all. Let us not forget that he advocated to the Welsh Rugby Union that a coach should be in sole charge of the national team and so do away with a selection panel – the so-called Big Five in Wales This was, of course, rejected either for being too radical or that it took away Power and Influence from the committee. In time the idea which was originally drafted in the 1970s as a condition if ever asked to coach Wales, was taken up twenty years later, in the 1990s. This proposal finally took root and is now the common practice.

This is as clear an example as any that Wales have failed to help shape events and have been cast instead as the grief stricken, the down-but-not-yet-out plaything of others. They have ineptly been unable to control events to their liking. There has been no leader. If Carwyn cut an unlikely figure as a leader, lacking the display and machismo associated with such a man, it was his understated style that mattered. He had the boldness of the kind philosophers enjoy; the confidence in words of rugby wisdom to which everyone interested in the game were always prepared to listen.

Carwyn's legacy should also have been the coach as innovator not imitator; of the quiet analysis of what is possible and, if needs be, to grasp at shadows; thinking always of what is promising; to think the unthinkable. "We are breeding robots," he once wrote. "We have few thinking players at the moment." Thinking is what he encouraged.

Carwyn explored the boundaries which he either expanded or contracted as he pleased or as the occasion and the players demanded. There was the afternoon in New Zealand when at training he asked us to do not just a single 'scissors' move, nor a double or a triple but a quadruple number. When it was suggested that we would never carry out such a manoeuvre on the field of play he replied: "But those New Zealanders on the touchline don't know that, do they?" He was referring to the contingent of 'spies' who watched our every move and reported back to the All Black camp.

"But, in any case," he went on with a smile on his face and his hair immaculately held in place, "Why not?" There was always time to spread a little mischief.

As well as the Lions he coached his beloved Llanelli to victory over the All Blacks in October 1972 and assisted the Barbarians to do the same a couple of months later. He took Llanelli to four consecutive Cup Final successes from 1973 while Rovigo under him won the Italian Championship.

When there was little more to prove he thereafter let his pen and his voice pass on the message in *The Guardian* and on the BBC in Wales. Writing may have been a chore for him: the tyranny of the clean sheet of paper first thing in the morning with which every writer is familiar. But the dilemma never came across in the final piece.

It is therefore so appropriate that a writer of sparkle and brilliance, a man who embraces words with affection, with every sentence rich and resonant in drawing the personality of Carwyn – the serious side as well as the mischievous whimsy in him – should have been inspired to delineate this vivid portrait. With his originality and wit Alun Richards has amused and enlightened us in his numerous novels, short stories and dramas. He knows the need of a strong narrative better than most of us. More than most the author understands the character of Wales and its people. He was a great friend of Carwyn's and came, outside the family, to understand him better than anyone. These qualities come together in Alun's 'personal memoir' which is simply the best evocation there is of this charismatic if restless man.

Carwyn had the humour and the common touch. He was modest and was a fine listener, an essential quality in a coach. He valued rugby as a team game but he valued it more for the distinctive and separate talents of players, which made up the team. He knew what he was doing and what he wanted to accomplish and how, in the friendliest, most companionable of ways, he could get others to trust him in his adventure. The art was in finding the design of the final cut.

Most amazingly of all is that after a couple of decades we should still wish to think of him and the contribution he made in particular to rugby, not just in Wales but on the world's stage. Rugby coaches like the rest of us have but a brief span. Only the blessed few are cherished. To this day Carwyn James is remembered whenever and wherever rugby is talked about.

If there were times when he did not say very much in company except for the occasional 'quite . . . quite', he might nonetheless care to have the last word. So it is the way we shall leave it here.

"Rugby football," he wrote in *The Guardian*, "should be played like living a life: fury and fun, chivalry and enjoyment – and for a shorter length of time than you'd like it to last."

Gerald Davies

Chapter One

The Flat on the Via I Monti

'Come to Italy?'

   I was not very keen.

   'Why not?'

   'Don't fancy it.'

   'Come on! I'll have a flat. You can work in the mornings. Rovigo's in the North.'

   'What's it like?'

   'Just like Llanelli!'

   'That rules it out then. If it was like Pontypridd, I might be tempted.' Where Welshmen are concerned, a blade of grass can form the frontier making foreign territory.

   'Come on! You'll like it when you get there. They're very friendly people.'

   'I'll see,' I said. 'Drop me a line when you arrive.'

   'That'll be the day,' a mutual friend said.

Carwyn James was notorious for his unanswered letters. At this time in 1977, although I had met him previously and known of him for most of my adult life, I did not really know him. He was a West Walian and I am an East Walian, and, as I was fond of telling him, we were as different as chalk and cheese. We had some things in common apart from a lifelong interest in rugby football. We had both been teachers, had both given up teaching – he, quite recently for journalism and broadcasting, whereas I had long since become a professional writer and, if I was known for anything in Wales, it was for my critical views of the Welsh Establishment. He, on the

1

other hand, apart from his differences with the Welsh Rugby
Union, was one of the most confident Welshmen of his
generation and moved easily in those Welsh-speaking areas
of Establishment Wales which, in my view, stubbornly refuse
to admit that there is no greater dividing line than that
formed by a language. It is a difficult thing to explain to an
outsider, how a man can feel a stranger in his own country,
and the indifference of many Welshmen to their nation springs
from the feeling, often justified, of being excluded, especially
from those organisations in broadcasting and education where
executive positions and a good many others are reserved for
those with bilingual qualifications. It is an old complaint, and a
lost battle as far as many Welshmen are concerned, but
Carwyn (who would not accept this view) was not only the
epitome of Welsh-speaking Wales, a Welsh scholar, a chapel
deacon and Plaid Cymru candidate, but an ex-Welsh-inter-
national fly-half, the triumphant coach of the 1971 British Lions
in New Zealand and a regular broadcaster who brought wit
and intelligence to bear on whatever subject he spoke about.
He was a man always in demand, who crossed dividing lines
with ease, and because of rugby football, one of the best-known
men in Wales.

'Rovigo's near Venice and Padua. It won't just be rugby.
There's the opera.'

'Duck-shooting as well, I expect?'

'Why not?

When Carwyn wanted something, he persisted. I did not
realise it at the time, but I see now that he was then a man
almost at the end of his tether. In the first place, it was a shock
to see how physically unfit he was – and his general health
never really improved. In the second, he felt a compulsion to
get away from Wales, to breathe a different air, and what was
to me a jaunt, was to him a need. He was going to be away for a
year at least and wanted company.

Always a convivial presence, he is somehow permanently
implanted in the memory, a glass in hand, wreathed in cigarette

smoke, his figure well-rounded, suit a little crumpled, sometimes lacking a belt, perhaps a remote Queensland rugby club
tie and shirt unbuttoned. It was as if he felt it was somehow
very English to be absolutely impeccable. Not that appearances
ever worried him, or those who most cared for him. It was his
smile which was the most important thing. When he smiled,
it was with his whole face, often nodding intently as if the smile
was not enough, and he had the most infectious chuckle.

'If I send you a wire, will you come?'

'I'll think about it,' I said. He was what is known as a
confirmed bachelor and I'd already had first-hand experience
of the domestic duties imposed on his guests, for he was a man
who regarded a tin opener as a complicated and highly
technical instrument, the use of which required at least a degree
in mechanical engineering. Once, at one of his many lodgings,
he had been charged with the care of a cat bearing the unlikely
name of Angharad Trenchard-Jones and, failing to open a tin
of cat food, had substituted the Sunday joint. I hesitated also
because I had a wife, children, and a novel to write.

But he rubbed his hands gleefully.

'Right! That's settled,' he said, as if a decision had been
made. The same invitation had been extended to a number of
people for he selected friends in much the same way a
bibliophile might choose books for his library – in all, a great
variety of people. He needed them all. But only a few came.
When I got to know him well, one of the first things to surprise
me was his vulnerability. In so many ways, he was a man who
could not say no to people, and there were days when everybody seemed to impose upon him and his time.

At that time nobody could understand why he wanted to
coach in Italy in the first place. As BBC Wales's rugby correspondent, his weekly match analyses on television were avidly
awaited. He wrote occasional elegant essays for the *Guardian*
on rugby football and had a summer brief to cover cricket. As
a journalist and broadcaster he was constantly in demand,
contributing to programmes of all kinds, and the summer

before, he had covered the Commonwealth Games in Canada for BBC Wales. He was also constantly being asked to speak at functions and wherever he stayed, the telephone never seemed to stop ringing. And yet he was bored.

Wherever he went, especially in rugby clubs and particularly in Llanelli, he was the subject of adulation. He could not walk down the street without being stopped by a host of people anxious to hear his views, often forcibly expressing their own on this rugby topic or that. At parties, he was the centrepiece, his ear the most easily purloined, for he was the most remarkable and patient listener ever. In short, he was the man everybody wanted to speak to and, although he was several times accused of arrogance in his dealings with the Welsh Rugby Union, he was really a lifelong victim of his own nature. For there was in him a sensitivity that made him the prey of other people, a gentleness of nature that did not want to offend, the capacity for which he secretly admired in other people.

A month later, contrary to expectation, both the letter and the telegram arrived. I soon found myself stepping off the plane in Venice to see his enigmatic figure smiling broadly down from the privileged visitors' gallery where he stood in the same suit and yet another rugby club tie, this time in the presence of two huge South African forwards, Dirk Naude and Dries Cotzer, guest players for his new club, Sanson Rovigo.

The customs formalities were soon over. 'You didn't expect the telegram, did you?'

'No,' I said.

'That's East Wales, you see? Suspicious, always.'

'Not without justification.'

'Never mind, now we can leave all that behind us.' But we never did.

I often reminded him of Joyce's phrase which I transposed – Wales is an old sow that eats her own farrow – but he always laughed. Of all the people he knew, he said, we were both the most easily available for the dish. Neither of us had ever stayed away for long. Neither of us could ever pass as coming from anywhere else, like some of our more famous compatriots whom we jocularly regarded as light-skinned negroes passing as white. In private such inflammatory phrases delighted him and we had a mutual habit of collecting sentences most likely to give offence. His favourite was spoken to me, a rebellious figure glaring over the wardroom silver in Portsmouth years before.

'There's something in what you say, Richards, and no doubt you have your contribution to make, however small!'

Such sentences delighted him, largely, I suspect, because they were the antithesis of himself.

In Venice, we took a launch to see the sights, but sitting in a café opposite the Basilica of San Marco he soon asked if I had brought the *Western Mail* as ordered and immediately turned to the Welsh rugby club results. He took his own square mile of Wales with him wherever he went and remained intensely rooted, Wales-centred and Wales-dominated. Yet, as I came to think, that inevitable preoccupation wore him out, whereas every contact outside of Wales stimulated in him the energy to return to the major obsession of his life, rugby football. Thus it was no surprise to learn that the one time he stood for election as a Nationalist Candidate, on the eve of the ballot he sat at the house of a friend, discussing his recent appointment as British Lions coach while the loudspeakers blared his name and party outside, his own presence denied his supporters for the evening.

Carwyn brought a Welsh eye to rugby football, he was the most unbiased of men and moved so freely amongst rugby men everywhere because he so seldom put a Welsh point of view. When Dai Francis, the General Secretary of the Welsh Miners, presented miners' lamps to the Welsh members of his Lions team and over-enthusiastically stated that the Lions would have been nothing without the Welsh contingent, he got himself roundly ticked off by their coach who insisted the victory had been won by a British team from all four countries.

In the game, Carwyn's intelligence transcended nationality, as did many of his views, but at the same time he was inescapably Welsh and you could not know him for long without hearing him quote his favourite poet, Gwenallt, bidding you remember that you cannot care for the nations of the world unless first you learn to care for your own.

All of which did not matter much to the Italians, nor indeed, I suspect, to most of the teams he coached, but wherever he went he was in some senses a permanent extension of a National Cultural Museum. The moment I entered his flat in Rovigo, it was to be greeted by sizeable portraits of the Welsh language writers who mattered most to him – Gwenallt, Kate Roberts, Saunders Lewis. On one occasion, hotly engaged in an argument in which I was expressing the anti-nationalist view, he promptly stood up and obscured one of my own books with a volume of Gwynfor Evans, the Nationalist MP, adding impishly, 'You were saying?'

Yet, as I was to discover, in personal terms Carwyn's nationality was the least important fact about him. The man who so confidently asserted himself on public platforms, on the television screen and in the rugby dressing-rooms of the world, was a man who came crisply alive on specific occasions and then afterwards relapsed into a wayward self when he seemed at times incapable of looking after himself and was, moreover, not much interested in whatever consequences befell him. There were thus two Carwyn James personas – the public man and the private man. They were markedly different. Neither was false, but it was sometimes impossible to believe that the one belonged to the other.

I was soon shocked to see how badly affected he was by the virulent form of eczema which haunted him all the time I knew him. He had a habit of rubbing his hands together, a brisk and vigorous movement as if to convey immense enthusiasm at the slightest provocation.

'Another g and t, Richards?' he might say in his naval voice. We had both served in the Royal Navy.

'Plenty of tonic.'

One of my favourites amongst his many stories concerned the taciturn English rugby captain in the dressing-room at Twickenham who had heard that the Welsh were giving lengthy team talks and, when it was suggested that he might do the same, reluctantly agreed. But he was a man short on words and, having called for silence, cleared his throat uneasily.

'Right, gentlemen! Today we are playing the Welsh, ahem.' There was an awkward pause while he struggled for the next sentence.

'All I can say is, we've got to beat the bastards!' A further pause.

'Er . . . has anybody here got a fag?'

End of team talk.

Carwyn told this many times always grinding his palms together as he did so, and it wasn't long before I realised that the skin on his palms was unnaturally hardened by this constant rubbing. In fact, there was not a part of his body that was unaffected by the eczema apart from his face. In the privacy of his flat, he couldn't wait to remove his shoes and socks. As the night wore on, that first night and every night after that, you could often hear him scratching in his sleep through the bedroom wall. He was to have various treatments, in hospital and out of it, including acupuncture, but nothing worked for long, although he never complained and ignored his condition so successfully that it embarrassed his friends more than it did him. This stoicism was an unexpected trait and his indifference to himself was matched only by his indifference to all possessions, from overcoats to suitcases to cars, all of which he abandoned when it suited him. To this day, I'm sure there are suitcases belonging to him dotted all over the world. He was a man who walked away from things and set no value upon them at all. 'Possessions' was an ugly word in his vocabulary.

Although no medical expert, I began by attempting to bully

him into taking more care of himself. Creams, lotions, powders littered the bathroom. More often than not, he forgot to apply them as if he had long since decided that he was the victim of an incurable condition. I urged cotton underclothes, air, light, vitamin C, the simple sensible things, but my concern bored him. There were things to do, people to visit, visitors to receive.

He had announced my arrival, making me a celebrity, and, as I soon found, a friend of Carwyn's was welcome anywhere. He had been installed in Rovigo for just under a month. His top-floor flat in the Via I Monti was just around the corner from the flat where the two South African forwards lived, the *stranieri* or foreign 'guest' players allowed by the Italian rugby authorities to each major club in order to further playing skills. They were his neighbours and friends, constant companions, and then there were the Rovigo team. The chairman, Franco Olivieri, had read of Carwyn and approached him through a previous *straniero*, Bernard Thomas, who had returned to play for Llanelli. The famous coach was already a minor deity and I was immediately accepted as part of his entourage. Carwyn was taking Italian lessons from Angelo Morello, a schoolmaster who lived around the corner, the most gentle of men who soon began to translate Carwyn's rugby articles for the local newspaper. I became *il companiato di rugby*.

It was like joining a potentate. Newly installed, I was assured by Franco Olivieri that my lack of Italian could be redressed by repeating *molto stupida*! whenever spoken to, a practice he himself found came naturally, as an ex-hooker like myself, and we shook hands on it in friendship. Indeed, friendship became the key note as we went from restaurant to restaurant and bar to bar, and once to a village nearby where a small rugby club had laid on a function to commemorate the death of their one international, a prop forward who had learned the game in Italy and then played at top level in France, returning home to have the local stadium named after him. In the little whitewashed tavern the local wine was produced in quantity. Carwyn and I sat bemused at the tributes and it suddenly dawned on me that I was in a rugby world as intense as any at home. Listening to the speeches of praise in memory of the fallen hero, I learned three more words of Italian – *aggressivo*, *generoso* and *combativo* – which gave me enough to be going on with. When Carwyn and I rose to sing the Welsh hymn, *Calon Lân*, there was tumultuous applause, before and after and the flashlights of cameras seemed only natural. Later that night we were in the cellar of a local property owner, inspecting his wine vats, and sat up so late talking rugby in broken English that his wife began to hurl abuse down the stairs. From that night on, transport, invitations, discount in leather goods stores, at the tailor's, and prize dishes in restaurants came our way like autumn leaves blowing down the Via I Monti itself. I had worked for Hollywood moguls and film stars and spied on showbiz extravagance, but these were the gifts of ordinary people, the whole town and, somehow, always more personal.

'It was,' I said, 'the Rugby High Life.'

'Why not?' Carwyn said.

The flat was headquarters – callers every day. They seldom came empty-handed. Players brought gifts of their family wine and some nights the whole team arrived, spreading themselves around the floor, often showing video films of previous matches until the cigarette smoke hung in the still air and the aggrieved faces of Saunders, Lewis and Gwenallt on the sideboard seemed to grow more and more grim and disapproving. The debris remained the following morning and Carwyn stepped through it without noticing. Twice a week a tiny woman came to clean, creeping in apprehensively, lowering her eyes as she entered, as if grateful not to find a hand or an arm, perhaps the odd finger, amongst the overflowing ash trays. Carwyn greeted her imperturbably with a warm smile and once, when she brought half a dozen crumpled shirts which he had forgotten to remove from the clothesline on the balcony – they had blown down and would have to be washed again, he grinned benignly. 'She is getting to know me!'

All the time I knew him, except when properly organised by his sister, Gwen, Carwyn lived like an artist, obsessed with whatever concerned him at the moment. When visitors from home were expected, all hands rallied round, but when left alone he soon created minor chaos for he was a marathon cigarette smoker of repute and gathered ash, unwashed glasses and debris around him like a walking Vesuvius. Often you could not get into his room because he filed the jackets of suits, blazers, sports coats on the toppermost edge of the door while the trousers blossomed like plants in the window or under the bed, or wherever they happened to fall. It was not just clothes. There were always letters, opened or unopened, their contents magically declared by the postmark, rugby programmes and currencies of all the rugby-playing countries of the world decorating the floor, the window ledge and odd niches, together with cheques, cashed and uncashed, as well as the four books he might happen to be reading simultaneously.

We had both been in the Royal Navy, so you would have thought we were used to keeping limited possessions tidy in cramped corners, but Carwyn's possessions seemed to multiply and spread. They began in his bedroom and extended like lava in a flow to the living-room, mounting chairs and tables, files mixing with shirts, ties, pieces of paper with training schedules and rugby diagrams as well as the usual crumpled envelopes on the backs of which he wrote lead paragraphs for his rugby articles. My first inclination was to turn housewife, but I suffered a setback early on. As a gift, I had brought several pounds of home-cured Mumbles bacon, the produce of a Mr Selwyn Shute.

'From his village,' Carwyn explained to the cleaning woman whom I had already designated for his rejected MBE. There were times when I caught her looking at me for sympathy, but I looked hastily away, and in all the time I was there she battled bravely on with startled eyes and the bemused stare of one who had wandered into the presence of gentle lunatics who, although not dangerous, were creatures from the planet of domestic chaos. Whenever she moved, she crept, picking her way delicately over this item of clothing or that, always treading carefully as if the place were mined and booby-trapped. Just before she left each day, she gave a wistful glance at the perfection she always achieved. It was, however, the glance of a pavement artist who knows that rain is inevitable. Carwyn always thanked her volubly and frequently pressed some of his gifts on to her, then looked over the balcony dreamily as she carried them down the outside stairs, some-times stopping for a life-saving return to sanity with a chat to the Italians downstairs.

But it was she who first heard of the advent of Mr Selwyn Shute's home-cured bacon which, in turn, became a conver-sation piece among our friends. The bringing of such a gift was easily understood and appreciated by the Italians who, like ourselves, came from small towns. Carwyn, whose Italian improved daily, had managed to convey that he was at heart a countryman, that his father had kept a pig and the killing of it was no small matter, indeed an occasion. He went on about it, quoting Gwenallt to such an extent that you would have thought I had brought the pig itself. Mr Shute was my grocer, I wanted to say; that was all. But soon it became a daily talking point, as, for one reason or other, usually too many invitations, several days passed before I prepared the meal. Even then I had to do so hastily in a growing temper: I had difficulties finding the utensils, operating the Italian cooker and finally getting Carwyn to the table on time while I juggled with the vegetables. I should say I was a Merchant Navy cook – 'chop and chips, spotted dick to follow!' – and by the time I had prepared three vegetables, there was a hint of over-cooking, even of mourning along the extra-crisp edges of Mr Shute's exported produce. We sat in silence, solemnly munching tinned celery, tinned sweet corn, a raffish touch of pineapple, also from a tin, and a few potatoes, the remainder decidedly singed. The occasion had been inflated so grotesquely that you felt people outside in the street might be interested, and once or twice, the woman below had come out on the steps to sniff as she looked upwards. When the doorbell rang, I went out of the kitchen to answer – Carwyn never opened doors if there was anyone else available to do it – and when I returned, the blackest portions had disappeared from his plate as he continued eating like a headmaster at the staff table. Later, I found his food neatly folded in a rugby programme, one of half a dozen on a ledge under the table. I had not done Mr Shute justice but neither of us referred to the matter again, and although I cooked again on many occasions, both he and the Italians were tactfully silent and I had the impression that he had asked them not to mention it.

It was an occasion of no particular import, except that like so many of the minor incidents in his life, it shows his inability to cause anyone pain, even the slightest reproach for something that was a joke. He had the most feminine of qualities that were unique in a brash, often combative masculine world and they made him hypersensitive to the feelings of others, a saintly quality which the Italians at once detected. Within a few weeks he was known as the sympathetic one, the man who never raised his voice and slowly, imperceptibly, he began to impress himself upon them. It soon occurred to me that rugby football was a long way away from his essential nature which seemed so far removed from the hurly burly of bruising games, the shouting crowds, the inflamed faces of spectators whose total identification with teams led from one unreason to another. You could not believe that he had played so successfully himself – a will o' the wisp avoiding the marauding hands of sizeable forwards like his lifelong friend Clem Thomas, or the formidable Pontypool destroyers of half-backs, Alan Forward and Ray Cale, this last a Dostoyevskyan figure, the most frightening forward I have ever seen on a rugby field, yet whom Carwyn always described as 'a perfect gentleman'.

With Carwyn inconsistencies multiplied, contradictions pre-sented themselves at every turn in his life, and while, in describing a friend, it is only too easy to fall into the trap of ascribing to him only the best of qualities, behind that quizzical countenance there was a divine spark that ignited fellow feeling like a reciprocal current in an uncanny way. Being vulnerable and sensitive, he was never a threat in any kind of relationship, but at the same time he had a rare gift that conveyed a special Carwyn empathy so that it sometimes seemed he magically made people grow on the spot. All who wanted to talk to him usually wanted something for them-selves for his presence so often enlarged a moment, and on those who mattered to him, he had an instant therapeutic effect in that they so often felt better for having met him. It was this *simpatico* presence which at first astounded the Italians. The constant cigarette smoking, the vicious skin infection, the travelling and ever-growing untidiness were further abrasions in a bourgeois world, but it was as if he rose from the ashes of inconsequential things to point a particular way, to get to the heart of any matter. The chaos was unimportant. When he wanted to, he had the gift of conveying the feeling that you mattered, you alone, and you in particular. It was not charm, and it was certainly not false, but an almost mystical com-munication of a rare kind from a man often given to long silences whose simple gift of getting the best out of people would never have been achieved without his lifelong habit of listening – an attribute which everyone who knew him well has remarked upon. It was, I discovered, a characteristic he had inherited from his father, a collier, who was also a private man.

Many famous Welshmen are rightly known for rhetoric, the forensic command of language that ignites those bonded in common cause, and in my lifetime I have heard most of them including Aneurin Bevan who had a masterly command of the language and always raised the tempo of the debate. He also had the gift of simplifying an issue with a deadly clarity.

He was at his best in attack, his voice and manner combining to wield sentences like scalpels: 'Mr Eden may be sincere, but if he is sincere, he is stupid, more of a fool than a knave, and in either capacity – we don't want him!' But Carwyn was not like this, seldom attacked, perhaps because he was a chapel-goer, never raised his voice and listened far more than he spoke. If there is one phrase to describe him in company, it is his persistent unobtrusiveness. He never pushed, and yet at times he seemed to be everywhere on the rugby scene, always with this charisma that left you with the feeling of uplift which was the hallmark of the most princely of his gifts – friendship. You seldom saw him without the feeling that he was glad to see you, that no matter how unexpected the encounter he had arrived specially to lighten your day.

Within a week of my arrival, it became clear that coaching days on Tuesdays and Thursdays were sacrosanct, and now he donned his tracksuit and went down to the stadium where the team assembled.

Rovigo, it should be said, was already one of the first-class Italian clubs, usually in the top three of the championship table, although one of Carwyn's first decisions was to re-arrange the three-quarters and to find a fly-half in the classic Welsh style, making the current fly-half a full-back, and then to find another with a quicker acceleration off the mark. Between the two players currently on offer to the club, it was simply a difference of length of leg and he wanted a shorter, more compact type of player who, despite his inexperience, he encouraged to call the moves. It wasn't difficult to see what he had in mind, for here, as in Wales, there was the difference between the natural instinctive runner and the 'made' player. Carwyn wanted the nervous intuitive instincts of a forest animal, as he used to say, and he was prepared to take chances, seeing the fly-half position, his own, as a key to his whole plan of attack, and soon he was insisting on maximum speed when a pass was given or taken. Most players begin their playing lives with the image of the player they most want to emulate and, as he knew, Bernard Thomas had been the hero of Rovigo and played some of his best games in Italy. So the fly-half position was crucial from the outset and this was the first change he made, treading on toes to do so, but insisting and making no compromise. When he wanted his own way, nothing would shift him. He could be adamant and decidedly inflexible.

During these training sessions, he kept his eye on the first and second teams as well as the schoolboys who assembled in the afternoons, his real working days. I hadn't forgotten that after he had taken over as Llanelli coach from his friend Ieuan Evans in 1969, Tommy David, 'Chico' Hopkins and J. J. Williams had mysteriously appeared in the Llanelli side, all drawn from other clubs.

'Are you buying or poaching this time?'

He did not reply.

I had read somewhere in the English press that his coaching task in Italy coincided with his appointment as a public relations officer for a firm making agricultural implements, principally tractors and, seeing an advertisement of a tractor driver in a magnificent set of outdoor oilskins, thought I might add to my wardrobe but when I asked him, he couldn't remember the name of the firm. It was not so much that his left hand did not know what the right was doing, but that it did not interest him.

Immediately there were other tasks, both on and off the field. He introduced a more sophisticated approach to the treatment of players and insisted that opposing teams should meet and drink together after matches, even though this wasn't common practice in Italy. Then committee meetings, meetings with the captain, the chairman and selected players, had a change of venue. I used to say that he was the man who introduced the high-class restaurant to rugby football and wherever he and his teams went, the quality of the hotels went up a star or two. He was also insistent on the provision of cars and drivers for those players who had to travel long distances – he believed in nothing but the best for his players. He expected it and he got it, even when it involved taking the wives of his Llanelli players on a Canadian tour.

Very soon, there was serious business. The All Blacks were to play their first ever game in Italy, stopping off on their way to a tour of France, and Carwyn was immediately asked to assist in the coaching of a President's XV which included several of his Rovigo players, among them the giant lock, Dirk Naude and, as two *stranieri* were allowed, Nelson Babrow, the Cape Town scrum-half. For this purpose, he alone went to Padua, but on the day before the match we attended a little ceremony where the President of the Italian rugby federation solemnly presented the team jerseys to the players. It seemed strange to have this ceremony on the day before but Carwyn approved. It cleared the officials and hangers-on out of the way a day sooner! The following day, joined by John Hopkins of *The Sunday Times* who had stayed overnight with us, we went to the match. Italy had only narrowly lost to Australia in Milan the previous year, but there were memories of a number of heavy defeats and, since this was the first visit of a New Zealand side, some apprehension could be expected.

The All Black side included Bryan Williams and young Stu' Wilson in the three-quarters, and Dalton, Haden and Laurie Knight among the forwards, a formidable combination. They had all greeted Carwyn in an earlier training session held at Rovigo when Carwyn's principal concern had been to secure enough silver fern brooches to supply the local committee and players, and then after that to queue with other fans to get the All Black players to sign a rugby ball. One minute, he was on the field advising Bryan Williams to stop raising his head as he took practice penalty shots, the next he was waiting at the exit to the changing-room, biro in hand. It was the kind of transformation of role I was to see many times. When the New Zealand forward, Brad Johnstone, joined us, we were transplanted back to 1946 when he told us that his father had been a member of the New Zealand Army Touring Team, the Kiwis, who were the first New Zealand team we had both seen. As an adolescent Carwyn had played at being the New Zealand wing, J. R. Sherratt, in playground games, the army wing having scooped up a mis-kick from the Welsh full-back and run fifty yards to score below a half-empty bomb-damaged stand. We agreed that the Kiwis were the most attractive New Zealand side we had ever seen, not the most formidable but certainly the most joyous, for there was a smiling quality to their rugby football personified by the impish Bob Scott at full-back whose duels with W. B. Cleaver in New Zealand several years after were recalled by another of Carwyn's friends, Terry McClean, much later. If the All Blacks were unfamiliar and feared by the Italians that day, they had been part of our growing up, and Carwyn often spoke about the Kiwis whose impact had lasted longer in the imagination than more effective and famous sides. They were the All Blacks who laughed, who played rugby for fun. It was the kind of rugby football he sometimes despaired of ever seeing again.

As we made our way to the Appian Stadium that morning, he drew my attention to the match poster which had just appeared. It was ominously all in black with a white centre-piece of a jinking player below the caption, XV Del Presidente (Italia) v. All Blacks (New Zealand).

Carwyn nodded at the player silhouetted in white.

'Know who that is?'

I didn't.

He grinned. It was Phil Bennett, the Welsh fly-half, an action shot taken up by an advertising agency and implanted in white upon the black background.

'An omen?'

He didn't think so.

As we approached the stadium there was none of the uneasy air of tension that seems to hang prayerfully in a pall over the approaches to the Cardiff Arms Park on international days. The fans were better dressed, altogether more exclusive-looking. They might have been going racing. Flowers hung in shapely baskets below the entrance, there were geraniums in a neat pattern set alongside an enclosed shrubbery. There was also a Tyrolean band in smart green uniforms, feathers in their hats, instruments of gleaming brass; in all, there was a carnival atmosphere. In matches, as a fan, I tended to identify with our own players and I had a puritanical and very Welsh view that this cheerfulness was misplaced, that we 'were going to get it!' as I told Carwyn, but he laughed once more. We had arrived early and before going into the dressing-room, he wanted to inspect the ground. It meant going down through the terraces. I did not want to, but he insisted.

'Come on!'

The ground was filling up rapidly. As the officials made way for us, I told him he was the most 'made-way for' man I had ever accompanied, including the film stars I had worked with. I felt self-conscious, would have much preferred to sit in the stand, making mischievous suggestions to the journalists. In the Llanelli clubhouse, Carwyn would disappear into private places, keep you waiting for ages and when you attempted to contact him, bodyguards would appear, look you up and down, and say that they'd see if he'd speak to you! I felt equally uneasy now.

'Come on!' he said again, challenging me.

As the officials unlocked the gates and we went through on to the field, I felt obliged to try and look important as I hurried after him. We went out into the centre of the pitch where faded soccer markings were still visible. As so often, I felt an imposter but he was laughing at me, teasing. I remembered the Welsh selectors of my youth in the days when they ran the line in suits, and at home big matches were always preceded by groups of notables walking slowly out to inspect the pitch as we schoolboys gazed down at them in awe. So I decided to become a notable. I lifted up my leg and gave a huge dig into the ground with my heel, then tested the direction of the wind by wetting my finger and holding it up. There were officials looking at us all the time, studying our faces. 'What was the plan, Signore?' The heel bit must have got to them. 'This is another man who knows!' When we walked back through the barricades people moved respectfully aside.

Carwyn looked back at me as I followed him.

'You walk like the Welsh Rugby Union!'

I never walked with him on these occasions, but behind him, like the man from the Pru'!

We went up to the changing-room, doors magically opening. Once inside, it became real. You could smell nerves as strongly as liniment. Grunts and nods had replaced speech. A huge masseur was busy at the table, there were one or two players standing singly or in corners, jumping up and down in private worlds, the noise of their studs on the terrazzo floor reaching a crescendo. I ducked into the showers but there was a player in there, fervently crossing himself in the corner. It was like a first night backstage: nerves, nerves, nerves! When Carwyn got to his feet to speak there was complete silence, but you could actually hear the distant sounds of the All Blacks moving ominously like horses pawing the ground in their stables in their dressing-room down the corridor. Carwyn took out a cigarette, lit it from the stub of a previous one, cleared his throat, looked around slowly, then assumed a ministerial role.

'Today we are playing against New Zealand,' he said loudly and clearly, 'a *great* rugby nation!'

It was all so totally unexpected, this praise for the enemy down the corridor. His authority was total and absolute. He had to pause while the South African scrum-half translated, his clipped accent chipping away at the Italian vowel sounds.

'For ten years,' Carwyn said, 'I played for my club, Llanelli, and never once did I have the honour of playing against them. I envy you your chance.'

He went on in this vein, emphasising the solemnity of the occasion, increasing its moment, but then he got down to details, ending, 'There is one man amongst you who has the key to this match . . .'

Here he paused and looked around and there was not a player present who did not feel his gaze. He was not talking about the stars, however (although they thought he was), and the team included the Francescato brothers, Bruno and Luigi, whom he came to regard as the best centre three-quarters then playing. Instead, he went up to a burly Brescia lock-forward and held him gently by the shoulder. This was the man who, as the principal line-out jumper's 'minder', he expected to give his all. He could expect to take more bumps than anyone else. Carwyn explained what he wanted, then took up his position by the door for the last handshake with each player before he went out. This was the guru at work.

If I had been surprised by his lack of fitness, the shock of the cruel unrelenting skin infection, amused by the waywardness of his general lack of organisation where he himself was concerned, now there was no doubt of his stature. His confidence was absolute. He attended meticulously to the details, the all-important ball winning, the clean possession required, the determination to run at the All Blacks. 'They never look so good going back!' he said. Then there was the need for discipline, and absolute silence on the field – not always respected in Italy. In those nervous moments, there could have been no other voice that was quite as sure. He had brought his reputation with him, yet he was not a large impressive person but simply a vulnerable one who knew. He was also a centre of calm. I had forgotten what young players were like, and how important it was for them to have someone who radiated confidence, and that was quite simply what he did – radiate. Standing there smiling, he watched them go one by one, the noise of their studs as they ran echoing on the concrete outside, and then they were gone. You had no doubt of Carwyn's presence.

At times, as I really got to know him, I must admit it occurred to me that he was too serious a man for rugby football which most people have the sanity to regard as no more than a game. But standing there that day, I saw a man who was doing what he wanted to do, and doing what he knew best. He so desperately wanted Italy to succeed, and identified totally with his young players. It was for them he wanted victory, and if not victory, honour. He'd had long chats with the regular coach of the side, and the three-quarters. He wanted Italy to be adventurous, to play, as he often put it, with the sun on their backs. He did not mind if they took chances. He was not worried by mistakes, provided they took the initiative. He had stern words for the forwards, there was going to be pain, but no one should go out on to that field without the conviction that the prize was in sight and within grasp. 'Do yourselves justice!' was one of his phrases and everybody seemed to take that to heart.

It is difficult now to read of the exhortations of some coaches without scepticism. Fred Allen, the famous New Zealand coach, was said to have invoked the spirit of Alamein in the dressing-room; Clive Rowlands, the Welsh coach, gave perorations at which few stood aloof, often exhorting players to think of their friends, their families, to feel proud as their representatives, all to mould a force of men. But Carwyn spoke to the individual: first he elevated the status of the opponents, then he pinpointed specific tasks like a rugby accountant with a ledger of expectations, ticking off points on the balance sheet. There was no suggestion of a performance and yet the way he spoke was masterly.

We took up our seats with the reserves. Impressed, I remained pessimistic.

'They won't get enough ball,' I said.

'Don't worry,' he grinned. 'The All Blacks will be on their best behaviour. It's their first game here – ever.'

And so it was an even match for a long while. When Italy took the lead after a lovely scissors movement, a classic move in the Bleddyn Williams mould, the excitement was electric. The chance was there all right, and there for the taking, but towards the end, the sheer power of that All Black pack asserted itself. Although Italy did not win, it was a narrow enough defeat for honour to be maintained. Then, after a quick congratulatory word in both dressing-rooms, Carwyn was eager to go. Boredom had already set in and as John Hopkins drove us to the match reception held at an inn high up in the mountains, he slept soundly.

I sometimes thought that he identified himself so completely with his teams that he scored every time his players scored, took every bump, felt every blow, received every admonition, and cursed every mistake. Matches in which he was closely concerned tired him and in this he was not unlike many of his countrymen who involve themselves so closely with players that they seem to emerge from grounds almost as exhausted.

At the dinner with the teams that night, he was barely interested and I discovered his outside-half's sleight of hand as he had a special gift for passing half a steak under the table cloth to his neighbour, a habit for which he was well known. The players were in high spirits, the speeches fulsome, the unending exchange of gifts, ties, brochures and silver ferns went on and on and the only time he showed a spark of his real self was when Jack Gleason, the New Zealand coach, expressed surprise that Carwyn and I were exactly the same age. He thought I was much older and, jokingly, we complained later of a breach of protocol to Ron Don, the New Zealand Team Manager. Instant alarm crossed his face like a grey shadow, revealing the kinds of problems he expected.

Once Carwyn left the dressing-room, he became lifeless, seemed out of place, but when we returned to the hotel he woke up again. And then in the weeks that followed, as one game after another took place and the winter began to set in, we were left more and more on our own in the nights when his duties left him free.

It was, I saw, a lonely life; the odd visits to the opera, the talks given to the sixth form of the local school, the chore of the weekly column when he would mischievously digress from rugby football and start by introducing obscure quotes from Welsh poets to perplex his readers who stood about at street corners and in the rugby bars puzzling – just as he had once done with the *Western Mail* – when fragments of a never-to-be-completed autobiography would appear incongruously, some of them revealing another self that yearned to express itself. Then his writing, like his conversation, would turn to

other matters, often literary, or to the political questions which
he frequently discussed. It would seem odd to me that the two
of us, both ultimately without political ambition, should be
hotly engaged in some discussion over matters which we
could scarcely influence so far away from home.

I took the view that the most effective contribution made by
Welsh politicians was always in London and, ironically, had
been made on the whole by men who had left school at
fourteen and received very little formal education; as the
opportunities for Welshmen increased and they became more
sophisticated, the more their contribution diminished. I was
frequently disappointed by the way the nationalist cause was
presented, although I much admired Gwynfor Evans's speeches
on the Vietnam question, copies of which Carwyn had with
him. Gwynfor Evans was right when nearly everyone else was
wrong and it was incomprehensible that Welshmen repre-
senting a small nation could not understand the struggle of
the Vietnamese people for freedom, or the reversal of roles of
the supposedly anti-colonialist powers which led to the deaths
of nearly a million children. Gwynfor Evans's phrase, 'That is
the most terrible thing that I ever heard of, and I come from
the country of Aberfan', struck at every one of us. We could,
and did, agree or disagree, and we burned plentiful midnight
oil as we aired the views which no one would ever hear.
Carwyn would walk about the room, pounding the floor endlessly with the result that the chairman of Rovigo, after
complaints from the occupants of the downstairs flat, tactfully
bought him a pair of slippers to soften his political footfalls.
Once, the doorbell rang at midnight to admit a wandering
South African lock-forward who wanted advice on the position
he was best suited for, and immediately we were back in the
familiar arena with Carwyn deploying the expertise which was
so sought after. It might be thought that these discussions have
no place in the memoir of a rugby personality, but it was rugby
football which brought Carwyn into contact with the Welsh
people as a whole, broadening his perspective. Yet he seemed

unable to increase the effectiveness of his simplistic arguments which failed again and again at the ballot box and certainly regarded himself as a failure in political terms.

Carwyn believed very strongly in the 'Welsh condition' and he saw it as important not only because he was so much a part of it, but because he thought of it as a condition that would spread. Wales's peril now might be England's in the next century since the structure of international capitalism and its concomitant high technology could mean that national minorities and small nations are swallowed up and swept aside and become too weak to offer any effective opposition. Like Saunders Lewis, he was convinced that the life and well-being of the Welsh language was a central political issue and he regarded the fight for its survival as a crucial aspect of the Welsh tradition, a matter that was totally incomprehensible to Welshmen who were not part of that tradition and never would be.

Welshmen have always had a choice between succeeding in England or remaining at home and it was ironically in Italy that Carwyn re-established himself as a home bird. He once quoted the Welsh novelist, Emyr Humphreys, who saw the choice for the able Welshman as being between magnetic poles, and was very conscious of a sense of guilt and sin among those who turned their backs on their own country. The poets and philosophers who peered from gilded frames were not there for any other reason than to reflect his admiration for those who had not been sidetracked from their aesthetic purposes and from whose influence he could never escape.

Yet although Carwyn was a miner's son who had once taken up the cudgels against the National Coal Board on behalf of his silicotic father, the names of Arthur Cook, Arthur Horner, Will Paynter and others which had been the most honoured names in the struggles of the Welsh miners in the Welsh coalfield, were almost foreign to him. Such men were not his heroes, in fact he had a marked distaste for those logrolling Tammany Hall politicians at a local level whom he forever associated with the Labour Party and also unreasonably blanketed with the Welsh Rugby Union despite its non-political nature. It was a matter of instinct rather than a sensible appraisal.

As I would tell him, somewhere along the line the landless laird of Cefneithin had acquired an aristocratic nose which was quite incongruous, an opinion I was to revise. Whereas so many nationalist politicians and writers tend to be remote figures, Carwyn was much in demand in all areas of Wales. He would have galvanised public platforms and audiences up and down the land had they heard him in full flight and a more convinced political animal would have seized the opportunity to do so.

But the opportunities he seized outside of rugby football, and his teaching, were openings that his fly-half's instinct divined, gaps in the defence that occupied him only for short bursts. He will be remembered by the multitudes as a superb rugby coach, by his ex-pupils as a gifted teacher, and most of all by his friends for whom he was a unique individual, gentle, caring and generous in gift and deed, very simply, as a good man.

When I left Italy after my first stay, he produced the rugby ball with the smudged signatures of the All Blacks, a bundle of tracksuits gathered like somebody else's washing from his widely distributed wardrobe – presents as ever for my children. I watched him standing with a Russian newspaper he had bought with the good intention of brushing up his Russian, a lone figure, dwarfed once more by his South African friends, and I realised I was coming away with a completely different impression of him. You could not be with Carwyn for long without realising the contradictions in his nature, but that was not all. There were parts of his nature which were mysterious for there was a remote part of himself which he kept quite separate, a retreat from which the often brash turmoil of the rugby world was barred and in which he thought his own private thoughts. As John Dawes, his Lions captain, said in an impromptu memorial tribute, 'He was able to stay on earth for a period of time, but then he'd be drifting into something else.' It was so true, and the answer really lay in those indefinable aspects of personality which, in his case, were only explicable in terms of his background. For me there was a touch of unworldliness about him, an unreason that could lead to the most extraordinary expectations. It led him to tackle the Welsh Rugby Union head-on with as little political nous as an eccentric feudal lord. And the inevitable rejection in turn led to an enormous heartfelt disappointment that sent him wandering across the world in search of active involvement in the game that occupied most of his life while at the same time he retained the romantic belief that his nation would call him back. This was one part of him, one strand in a complex web; the other was more curious still and is best explained by a comic incident which occurred some years after my first visit to Italy.

Once, while he was away, he left his car awkwardly parked outside my house, causing great inconvenience for nearly five weeks. When he returned unannounced to pick it up, before I could say anything he raised his head gravely, opened the boot and solemnly presented me with a loaf of home-baked bread and half a pound of salted farm butter as a reward. After five weeks, you could have converted neither, but at the instant of handing over the gift there was in his eyes an intensity of expression and a solemnity of purpose that saw not the slightest humour in the situation. In that instant you would have thought, as the result of a single, silent command, the bacteria retreated in close order. It was not so entirely, but there was always the chance that it might have been true. There was, after all, something of Merlin in him – the enchanter and counsellor of Arthurian romance said to have strange powers of divination. Merlin, we are told, is a composite figure of diverse traditions: on the one side of human parentage, on the other demonaic, and perhaps it is no accident that in Carwyn's whole life no words more completely sum him up than enchanter and counsellor. Who, in all the hundred years of rugby reportage could pick on such a doughty warrior as Llanelli's Ray Gravell and describe him to the readers of the *Guardian* as belonging spiritually to the army of the last real Prince of Wales, Llewellyn the Last? Llewellyn died in 1282, killed, not in Cefneithin or Rhydlewis but in Builth Wells (colours: black and amber).

But such realities made no difference to Carwyn for whom the future in so many ways was but the past, seen through another door; a view from another direction which merely called itself the present. In everything he did or said, there was always a hint of disparagement at the boredom of merely reasonable behaviour.

Chapter Two

The Countryman Collier

In Wales there are two languages, the Welsh and the English, and in Carwyn James's life the Welsh language was central, the language of his heart and hearth. Nothing would shift him from his adherence to its cause and those who supported it – no historical fact, nor any opposing point of view expressing even a mild indifference. If he understood facts, he did not necessarily pay attention to them and on this issue he would never budge: Wales *was* the Language, the Language *was* Wales. Without it, you were a lesser person, and while the logical thing was to advocate it be promptly learned, he would some-times confess to a certain unease in the presence of those persons who had actually done all he said they should do since they tended to assume slightly artificial postures and were almost inevitably off-centre in the company of natural indigenous Welsh-speakers. You could not win, I would tell him, and at times it was as if he recognised this and regarded his own inheritance and fluent command of the language rather as an aristocratic landowner might regard acres of land which had been held in the family for centuries – as if such felicity was a matter of breeding and, do what you might, you could never really and completely acquire breeding. Secretly, I am sure he was just as haughty as that and the Welsh language, I came to understand, was the reason for many of his attitudes which, while they might appear incongruous in the son of a coal miner, were nevertheless explicable in that he never spoke quite like the son of a working man and so, in his case, the Marxist hypotheses fell away like chaff and gave him the kind of classlessness that is otherwise totally absent in English society. There were reasons for this, accidents of geography and good luck, and a family history that was marginally different from that of the common run.

In the general exodus from countryside to town, the ancestors of most of the indigenous Welsh exchanged their culture and language for English which, until the rise of Welsh Nationalism, was generally regarded as sensible, being the simplest road to economic survival. It was true of Dylan Thomas's Carmarthenshire antecedents, as it was of my own. To so many of our grandparents, the Welsh language was the language of the hearth and the chapel, but the English language was the key to prosperity and commerce, the white bread to be gravely weighed against the brown. The result so often was that the Welsh language came for the children and grandchildren to have something of a precious quality in the Welsh novelist Gwyn Thomas's words, 'To have the status of a pet, reserved for occasional greetings' – a Sundays-only language which was useful for conversations when it was desirable 'to keep things from the children'.

In my own case, it was very definitely my grandparents' language and had a special Sundays-only significance since they attended a nonconformist chapel. For most of my childhood, the Welsh language was part of a past which bore no relation to the world in which I lived, and if I saw it as belonging to anything, it was to the chapel itself – in a state of decline, weak, ailing and defenceless in a world which grew more violent every day. To so many of us in the eastern valleys of Wales, the Welsh language was the language of *old* people and those young people who spoke it were in some way freaks, either very recent immigrants from the rural areas of Wales or, often, the sons and daughters of nonconformist ministers who maintained stubborn oases of Welshness which seemed somehow comic and countryfied to outsiders. This was often reinforced by endless valley jokes in broken English about such characters as Ianto Full Pelt, and *Dai*-stories in which barely articulate Welshmen were portrayed as stupid or *twp*, perhaps sly into the bargain and, unfairly and illogically, the two views often merged together.

The language seemed to many of my generation to have no part in our lives and we rejected it without a thought, a process in which we were encouraged by the fact that even in school the Welsh language had a somewhat dowdy status compared to Latin, the mastery of which, it was often implied, would almost assure you of a place in medical school. There was, of course, St David's Day, a half holiday and a morning concert, leeks and tall hats to the fore, and it was usually on this occasion that most of us made our first appearance in the local paper, listed as soloists or part-singers in a prize-winning group singing Welsh songs we could barely understand; or again, in one of the interminable comic sketches in which a Welsh dentist might extract a Welsh tooth and large root (in the shape of a Welsh carrot) to such exclamations as '*Darro!*', or similar vernacular words which remained with us for the rest of our lives.

It was all part of Shakespeare's 'insubstantial pageant' and most of us in the Welsh valleys and cities were already looking for an escape anyway; and those of us who grew up in the war were ever aware of a larger world beckoning to us on every hand. Even those born in comparatively affluent circumstances were aware of the long lines of the unemployed threading their way in shabby queues along the main street, while no one who attended a council school in the 'thirties could be unaware of malnutrition, of leg-irons masking rickets, and the sight of undernourished, ragged children shivering damply in inadequate playground shelters in the winter when it seemed to rain incessantly. Before we were into our teens, the war came: a convulsion of national purpose, and then casualties, telegrams to next-of-kin, rationing and shortage, a universal exhortation to 'stick it out', and at no time in our lives did an ancient language, for the most part abandoned by our parents, seem of the slightest importance.

This was a common experience for most South Walians but it was not Carwyn James's experience, nor that of his contemporaries who lived in areas on the periphery of the coalfield which had been unaffected by the large-scale immigration of Englishmen and others in the decades which followed the exploitation of the coal industry. In Carwyn's case, from the moment of his birth in November 1929 in Cefneithin, a small industrial village about ten miles from Carmarthen in the Gwendraeth Valley, he was surrounded by people to whom Welsh was the first language and who, for the most part, would have considered it unnatural to speak any other, unless to strangers or employers. In Carwyn's case also, there was a further complication, indeed a whole series, since the family's roots had in 1929 only very recently been removed from the countryside proper, from the Cardiganshire village of Rhydlewis where they could trace their ancestry back to the early eighteenth century. In the matter of language this was important, since Carwyn was not encouraged to speak a Welsh tongue tainted with the industrialised dialect of Cefneithin, but the purer Welsh of his parents' county; and he, like his brother, Dewi, was corrected when he spoke in the vernacular. It is a simple point, but it explains a multitude of things and, moreover, the family was descended from the Welsh bard Rhys Dyfed (1837-66) of whom *The Dictionary of Welsh Biography* records, 'He took every opportunity to culture himself and master the English.' But he still wrote in Welsh, winning prizes in eisteddfodau and, like his descendants, remained firmly rooted in his Cardiganshire past. This was an important reality in the life of the James family for, as Carwyn's brother relates, as children they tended to know people in the Cardigan village of Rhydlewis more intimately than in Carmarthenshire's Cefneithin for it was smaller, with a longer standing cohesion, and indeed they visited it frequently and could point to the houses of parents, grandparents and family which had been continuously occupied for over a century. In Carwyn's mind, Rhydlewis was Avalon, the country of the heart, a Welsh Elysium.

In many ways, this connection was untypical since migrating families tended over the generations to lose touch with their country roots but there was no drift to new ways, except that Carwyn's father, Michael, made a gradual change. Born in 1891 in Rhydlewis, he left primary school at fourteen to work as a farm labourer and occasional carpenter like his ancestors, one of whom had been a builder of substance whose properties stand to this day. Michael James was one of five brothers, all of whom were eventually forced to seek work elsewhere, mostly in South Wales (one eventually emigrated to Australia in the 1920s where he became a draughtsman with the Sydney City Council). Michael James travelled the shortest distance, to Cefneithin, where he first lodged with a Congregationalist minister who had worked as a miner. He began work at Cross Hands Colliery in 1921, travelling home to his native village at weekends, and he was already married with three of his children born in Rhydlewis when he finally moved and set up house at Cefneithin in 1927. Of his four children, Gwen (born 1914), Eilonwy (born 1918), Dewi (born 1927), only Carwyn was born in Cefneithin, in 1929, and he was to write:

> I often wondered whether I would have played rugby football at all had I been born in Rhydlewis and had lived there as a child and a young man. My father left the farm and came to work as a miner in the Gwendraeth Valley, and so, like Dai Hughes and later Barry John, like most of the boys living in the village of Cefneithin, I was doomed to play rugby.

The use of the word doomed is perhaps careless, but in other unpublished autobiographical sketches there is evidence of strain and more than a suggestion of the complex individual who would pound the Italian floor with his obsession with Welsh concerns.

In the last few years of his life, he thought of buying a house in Rhydlewis and loved to return there, perhaps because he realised that the Rhydlewis connection had turned out to be such a healthy one for his family. Not only was the family guaranteed holidays, but they were part of the rich life of an older village community in which they and their family had always been well regarded. There was a general store which housed the grocer, shoemaker and barber (all with the same pair of hands) and formed a community centre, together with a hall which housed a snooker table and where Saturday films were shown. Here the local boys would wait for their recently emigrated friends to arrive on the weekend bus.

The family connection also provided an economic advantage. In 1925 the anthracite coalfield was convulsed with a strike and labour disturbances in a localised struggle by thirty thousand miners who fought to protect long-established customs like the seniority rule which was a unique feature of the anthracite district. Now described as a forgotten strike and overshadowed by the General Strike and Lockout of 1926 which lasted for almost a year, the cause of the anthracite strike illustrates a further difference between East and West Wales.

The coalfield in which Michael James worked in the 1920s was dominated by drifts and small levels owned by local farmers or 'self-improved' miners, supported by a mining engineer, a foreman and occasionally by additional capital from 'leading' members of the village.

> The mines were sufficiently small for recruitment to be limited to the immediate locality and consequently were very much village enterprises. The owner was known intimately by his employees as he had probably attended the same elementary school, Sunday school and continued to frequent the same chapel and the public house, was part of a shared community experience of individual anthracite villages and such grievances could be more easily resolved within such a context. Discontent with economic hardships and conditions must have been appreciated by the owner to the extent that he respected

the miners' customs and did not normally challenge them. Similarly, the owner was content to receive a relatively moderate and leisurely return on his money and was not answerable to a large and alien body of directors and shareholders, demanding ever increasing returns. The custom of the 'Seniority Rule' grew out of such an enclosed society. When the coal trade temporarily fell off in the summer months miners were allowed to migrate to the adjoining steam coalfield and return later to claim their old workplaces. Similarly, a miner could not be laid off at the discretion of the manager: he was protected by his date of employment and those most recently employed would be the first to be made redundant.*

This was to lead to a direct comparison between the coalfields of the East and West, for the combines of employers first established in the East formed a formidable organisational machine in which the worker was merely a cog. Although this system was beginning to operate in the anthracite coalfield in the 1920s, mass unemployment and starvation wages were never a feature of life in the West as they were in the East.

Dai Dan Evans, General Secretary of the South Wales Miners, made a further distinction:

> The difference between the leader and the ordinary rank and filer in the anthracite area is much less than in the steam coal. In the anthracite area, if you wanted to dismiss a man who was a bit of a troublemaker, they would have to take possibly a hundred men out before him (because of the Seniority Rule). Consequently, you see, you had lambs roaring like lions in the anthracite, but they had to be a lion to bloody well roar like a lion in the steam coalfield.

---

* Hywel Francis, 'The Anthracite Strike and Disturbances of 1925', *Llafur*, Vol. 1, No. 2, 1973.

But Michael James, neither lamb nor lion, went his own way. He is described as a quiet and private man, a careful craftsman and a good listener, and he had his own solution to the disturbances and strikes of the 1920s. He could always find some employment in Rhydlewis where his skills with his hands as carpenter and farmer were sufficient to help support his family at a difficult time. Cefneithin was markedly different from other mining villages even in the same coalfield like Cae'rlan where Dai Dan Evans, born some seven years later than Michael James, recalls:

> There was not a single boy from my village in the county school which was about three˙miles from where I lived. The old master in the village school, Richard John Lewis, tried to coax me to sit the examination but I wouldn't do it. Mother coaxed me, too. You must remember that all the young lads at the time were steeped in mining. The only conversation you could get in the community was about mining. You were trained for the pit and nothing else.

This was an industrial experience that differed significantly from the more rural western valleys of the coalfield and it was one that led to another way of life, to ideas and views which were to create other kinds of Welshmen more open to the prevailing political winds of the 1920s. Where life was harder, views were less flexible and it is inconceivable that the scarlet banner stitched with gold leaf that the women workers of Moscow had presented to A. J. Cook of the Rhondda in the lock-out of 1926 (when Cook had gone to seek assistance for his members from the Soviet Union) could have found its way to Cefneithin. It went to Maerdy, 'Red' Rhondda's little Moscow. But the Rhondda was a different society, made different by immigrants who soon began to outnumber the indigenous Welsh population. It was not long before, as in Dai Dan Evans's case, families knew none other than the industrial way of life. In the James family, the Rhydlewis connection with the Cardiganshire countryside meant they experienced an older way of life and, importantly in the early life of Carwyn, not only was the quality of life more varied, but it was carried on in the traditions of the Welsh countryside and the Congregational Chapel which meant a veneration for learning and scholarship. Michael James was the only one of his family who went underground and he did not do that until he was nearly thirty, then working continuously until 1945. Indeed, he always regarded his late entry into the mining industry as a benefaction since he was less exposed to the risks of pneumoconiosis than those Cefneithin contemporaries who began at fourteen. Many of them died wholly crippled by lung diseases, whereas he himself, although partially disabled, lived until he was 81.

When the James family settled in Rose Villa, a three-bed-roomed, semi-detached cottage which they rented from a neighbour, they brought other country skills to the industrial village. They had a narrow garden of enormous length which backed on to the local rugby pitch and was long enough to house a pig, once a turkey, and a fair share of produce, so Michael James was able to carry on the smallholder's traditions both at home and on neighbouring farms where his skill in making ricks was traded for sour milk and scraps to feed his livestock. The picture was one of a countryman's continuing industry with hams hanging in the kitchen, prize onions grown for display, the daily shift work at the coalface being the only interruption in a way of life that had remained the same for centuries. The rent of seven shillings and sixpence a week remained virtually the same for nearly thirty years. Anne James, the mother of the four children, had a bank account, a rare enough achievement for a collier's wife in the 1930s. The two girls, Gwen and Eilonwy, were destined for nursing careers and began to contribute to the family income from an early age so that by the outbreak of war, when the family had reached the height of their prosperity, both the sons, Dewi and Carwyn, were being raised in relative comfort and there was no question but that both should seek higher education, urged on by their mother and with the financial support of the whole family.

Mrs James read to the children from the popular romantic novels of Moelona, a Welsh novelist born in Rhydlewis, and much disapproved of the satirical portraits in the stories of Caradoc Evans, Rhydlewis's most famous writer in English who was to scandalise his nation with venial tales of the Welsh peasantry. Even so, a copy of his book, *My People*, was kept on the bookshelf, probably because the family felt they could identify the source material. There is nothing Welsh people like more than an inside story.

Outside the house, the chapel formed the hub of a closeknit family life in which the separate tasks of each member of the family seemed, however, to exclude the youngest who was to be the recipient of all the family's attention. He was, in fact, the only one of his family not to be named after a relative like his brother and sisters: he bore the name of a nearby minister's son who had died in infancy several weeks before Carwyn's birth. In the never-to-be completed autobiography, he wrote sketches of his childhood which give a picture of some of the poignant moments in his early life, all revealing a sensitivity which he retained throughout his adult life.

> I'm afraid to watch on my own lest I fall off the gap in the hedge, my hiding place, onto the playing field, and I don't like the stinging nettles. I plead with my father to stop working in the garden, to stop admiring the grunting pig and to take me to watch the 'beetball'. I hold his large, warm, collier's hand and I feel safe, and I watch the huge men throwing the ball around. I enjoy watching them and I think my father does too, perhaps only because his three-year-old son is so quiet. I don't like to hear the people shouting. Their voices, coarse and primitive, frighten me.

One memory was followed by others, all as fragile as leaves.

> I go to school early in the morning. The council school
> in Cefneithin, a little village near Llanelli. Viv, Gwyn and
> Llyn are already there and we play soccer with a small,
> soft ball on the hard playground. The smallest and the
> youngest, I play with Cliff because he is bigger and older
> but we lose. I loathe playtime. I have to drink milk, which
> I hate, so I stuff my mouth with chocolate biscuits before
> gulping the cold milk down. I feel sick. I lose most of my
> break and most of the game and I'm very angry. I sulk
> in the lesson; refuse to listen to Miss Jones, Standard
> Two, who in her anger raps me on the knuckles.

*   *   *

> Every evening after school we play on our road, Heol
> yr Ysgol (School Road), two brothers versus two brothers.
> Meirion, the eldest and I, the youngest, against our
> brothers Dewi and Euros. We play touch rugby but, as
> always, touch becomes tackle. We quarrel. Meirion fights
> Euros, and I kick Dewi on the shins, before bolting to
> hide in the *cwtsh-dan-star* (hole under the stairs). In the
> afternoon we play again and sometimes I can beat them
> with a side-step. I believe I'm Haydn Top-y-Tyle or
> Bleddyn Williams. I love these games, but especially I
> love playing cricket on the road, for the ball somehow
> grips better on the road and I can bowl Peter round his
> legs. I think I'm Doug Wright and occasionally I'm Johnny
> Clay, but although I bowl better when I'm Doug Wright,
> I support Glamorgan and a photo of the team hangs in
> my bedroom.

*   *   *

> Iestyn James, one of my heroes, is out practising his
> place-kicking. I can hear the thud of the ball on the hard
> ground. I join him. He is a tall man with fair, wavy hair,
> and freckles, and for the occasion he wears large, brown

shoes and has a kick like a mule. Standing behind the goal posts, miles from Iestyn, I try to catch the ball before it bounces and then I use all my strength to kick it back to him. I'm pleased when he says that one day I shall play for Cefneithin.

*   *   *

Today it is our neighbours, Rhys and Menna's turn to kill the pig, so their uncle J.P., is there, fretful and fussy, to cast a critical eye on the operation. Soon we shall have the bladder to play rugby, and faggots for supper. I hate the killing. Hiding behind my brother, I'm drawn by fear to peep round his legs, fearful, even while eager to see. How I despise Wil y Mochwr for his sharp knife, his butcher's apron, his boiling water, his scraper which I shall hear and feel for a long time to come, perhaps for ever. I despise him even more for his not being afraid. The fat fat creature, overfed by a few score pounds maintains a piercing, high-pitched screech as he fights for life. His hind legs hang from the ceiling in a vanquished 'V' formation; his warm, red blood drips on the cold, stone floor. It is all over, he is as dead as the last one. Suddenly, in defiance of death, he twitches and I run away.

*   *   *

I'm nine. A Saturday afternoon in late March and Cefneithin are at home to Trimsaran. My job is to recover the ball from the gardens. The gardens are neat and tidy, and I've had strict orders from Dad and the neighbours to tread gently and to avoid the onion beds during the match. The touchline which I guard is only a yard from the hedge protecting the gardens, so usually I'm kept busy. This afternoon is no exception as Trimsaran play to their forwards, and their halves kick a lot. Geraint, our fly-half, is playing well, whilst on two occasions, running like a corkscrew, Haydn Top-y-Tyle almost scores. He eventually does and in my excitement I fall and I'm stung by the nettles. I swear under my breath as I get back on my perch just in time to see Iestyn converting from the touchline. The Trimsaran full-back drops a lucky goal but we win by five points to four. I dash on to the field to collect the balls and to pat the players on the back as they make their way to the School to bath in the small tubs. I accept my threepenny bit from Dai Lewis, the Ironmonger, who is the club secretary and I look forward to spending it later in Eunice's fish-and-chip shop, which is opposite the Public Hall.

*   *   *

I'm ten and in Standard Four. The war is on, we have gas masks in cardboard boxes, air-raid shelters in the gardens, and a talented dad's army in the village of which my father, trained as a marksman on rabbits in Cardiganshire, is a devoted member. I read 'Rockfist Rogan, RAF', in the *Adventure*. It is Monday morning. Suddenly, in the middle of sums, at eleven o'clock exactly, the hooters of Cross Hands, Blaenhirwaun and Tumble collieries combine like massed brass bands at the National to sound the alarm, and at the sharp command of Miss Rachel Ann Jones we dive dutifully under our desks, so we miss all the fun. For a German bomber, flying very low, is driven by a Spitfire towards the sea at Cefn Sidan. The Germans panic and drop their bombs over Gwendraeth Grammar School, just off target, fortunately, so no one is hurt. That night as I listen to my friend Aeron, an eyewitness, bragging about what he had seen, I'm consumed with envy, feeling cheated of a memorable experience, of witnessing with my own eyes the skill of a Rockfist Rogan shepherding his prey, a real German bomber, to the kill. To be a pilot, a fighter pilot, is now my only ambition – Goering is the enemy, God is on our side (the Minister told us so yesterday) and we dutifully hang 'our washing on the Siegfried line' every

Monday. I don't sleep well, for I plunge bomber after bomber into the sea at Cefn Sidan. How I long for the war to last until I'm old enough to join the RAF.

*   *   *

Cricket on the road and I'm batting. The ball runs down the hill from an immaculate Emrys Davies drive over the bowler's head. An ambulance, the one vehicle feared by a miner's son, turns the corner and is coming towards us. We step onto the pavement. I can feel the uneasy silence. The dreaded ambulance comes slowly up the slope, over the pitch and the three stones, our wickets, and, at last, passes my home. From relief I hit the next ball wildly on the leg side into Ffynnon-cawr's hayfield; and I'm out.

*   *   *

In Standard Five my favourite afternoon is Friday, an afternoon of drama, music and games. I like mime and drama except when the teacher asks me to do something on my own in front of the class. I feel proud that our teacher, Mr Evans (we call him Gwyn Shop behind his back because his parents run the combined post office and shop opposite the school), writes plays and is a drama producer. He also helps Cecil James, a fine local musician, to produce operas and once I was invited to take part in Smetana's, *The Bartered Bride*. I thus prefer the Welfare Hall to the Cinema, and I often go with my mother to the Hall to see the plays of Dan Mathews, Edna Bonnell, Gwynne D. Evans and Emlyn Williams, and on one memorable occasion I even went to see Lewis Casson and Sybil Thorndyke.

*   *   *

Mr Jones, the schoolmaster, is strict and we have to develop a liking for the modulator because he likes the modulator. We touch the notes gently to lah as we race

up and down the ladder, and then, at the command of
his ruler, we leap dangerously from doh to soh to doh
and leap down again. W.J. is enjoying himself, already
seeing in us members of the choral society singing
'Worthy', or 'Man is born of woman', but the boys are
just holding on, producing half-hearted, almost inaudible
treble notes in case he detects a wrong one. How we
pray that we are not made to sing on our own, and long
for the afternoon break, for the games lesson is to follow.
The modulator, even, grows on one and I have it in the
Band of Hope on Tuesday as well. I have to practise sol-fa
at home, for Dat, who sings for the village Male Voice,
communicates in sol-fa with the confident air of a man
conversing in his mother tongue, and insists that I read
the tenor line to harmonise with his bass. I enjoy listening
to the Male Voice, and often on a Saturday night I lend
my support at an eisteddfod, feeling so proud when I
watch my father, Lloyd Low, 'W.J.', and the demonstrative
conductor, Tom Asa Williams, the barber, singing
'Comrades in Arms'. How eagerly I long for them to
win, which they usually do.

*   *   *

Gwynne D. Evans is an all-round sportsman while W.J.
Jones played for Llanelli and had one cap for Wales as a
hooker. I love the games lessons, particularly when we
play rugby, for like W.J. I also want to play for Wales.

This was Carwyn, small, protected, who sometimes ran home
from school at playtime because he could not wait to read of
the adventures of Rupert the Bear, a cartoon serialised in the
Daily Express, the same Carwyn who at nine trooped into his
parents' bedroom on Christmas morning to be asked what he
thought of his Christmas present. He had been given an
insignificant trifle when he wanted a portable gramophone
and replied in Welsh with the addition of a singular local
adjective that had crept unknown into his vocabulary, 'What
a fucking present I've got!' The imp had not yet become the

athlete, was not yet as he put it, 'doomed to play rugby,' and had not yet returned home, his pockets jingling with silver coins, having scored a century for the nearby mining village of Tumble, the colliers watching and having an immediate collection 'for the schoolboy'. In primary school, his headmaster, W. J. Jones, was an ex-international rugby player 'but never spoke about it', and if the little school was known for anything, it was the excellence of its mathematics teaching. The medium of instruction was English and Carwyn only ever talked of his schooldays with affection.

But for all its rural atmosphere, Cefneithin was a pit village and every day when he came home from school, he would pass his father's workmates, helmeted and pit-black. And there were other harsh realities, at first puzzles, to be understood.

I attend my first funeral, a large funeral composed of men only, consequently the singing is loud, incredibly loud even for a chapel, and I feel small, glad that my father is with me. I look around the gallery of dark suits, white collars and black ties, and I'm compelled to count the blue and black scars on the faces and on the large hands holding the white pamphlets; I count Dat's as well.

I feel sorry for John, Mair, and David, crying in the front row of the mourners, but when the Reverend Llewelyn Jones refers to the passing of a young man, I don't understand, for I look at the pamphlet again and find that he was quite old. He was 36. We leave the chapel and stand outside and while my father lights his Woodbine I listen to two miners I had never seen before.

'Pity. Full of silicosis, poor chap, and so young.'

'Let's hope his wife gets Compo.' (Compensation awarded to a miner's wife if the post mortem shows that he died of silicosis. Too often it doesn't.)

'Ay, more than his mother did. Old Ianto was full of it, too, but they said he died of a heart condition. A bloody heart condition, I ask you. And there are hundreds like him.'

'It's about time *they* did something about it.'

As we walk home quietly I wonder who 'they' are, and
since Dat won't tell me I don't understand, and so I start
counting them by the hundreds. By the time I have
reached fifty we are home, tea is ready, and I forget the
hundreds. And I soon forget John and Mair and David's
father . . . and mother. I'm no better than 'they'. Perhaps
Dat won't get silicosis.

It was to be a vain hope but his father's late entry into the pit
and his considerable skills as a craftsman protected him and
those who worked with him. Peter Rees, later a Welsh international three-quarter and now President of Llanelli Rugby
Club, worked with Michael James as a boy and recalled his
careful ways underground, adding, 'When you finished a stint
with him, you knew you had done a day's work!' He was
fatherly to his young helpers, always quiet, a fair man, 'a bit
on the religious side', much respected but in all things a private
person.

It is clear he did not bring the colliery and its problems home
with him and he traditionally handed over the whole of his
wage packet, sometimes asking his wife for half a crown to be
returned on a Saturday to give an additional reward to the
boys who had worked with him during the week.

For Carwyn it was a happy childhood and one extra source
of his happiness were the visits home of his sister Gwen, then
a nursing sister in Gloucester, whom he was sent to meet at
the bus stop and from whom he was to receive special
attention all his life. Once, when Gwen had neglected to write
home after a long period of night duty, their mother became
concerned and sent an anxious telegram, but Carwyn assured
her that she could not be dead yet as 'she was not married', a
peculiar piece of logic. He seems to have been full of these
deductions for on another occasion, annoyed to find his sister
descend from the bus with her suitcase being carried by a
stranger, he was sufficiently perplexed to ask himself why and

concluded that it was because she was wearing a new hat with a bundle of artificial cherries, and of which he did not approve. It is not difficult to imagine Carwyn in these years, untroubled, basking in the glow of everyone's affection. It was an early experience that was, so far as his intimates were concerned, to last him all his life. The cherished son was to become the cherished man.

Chapter Three

How many BAs have we got who can drop kick?

Memories of schooldays tend on the whole to be written by the successful and in recall a hazy glow is often cast. This is also true of the celebratory publications collated for special occasions like school jubilees. The founders are recalled, the optimistic hopes of local worthies related and demonstrated as achieved where possible, notables pumped for complimentary memoirs and gratitude is everywhere, a general benign feeling of satisfaction collectively bestowing the blessing of rosy cheeks upon even the palest of skins. The general theme is always, Forward with the School! Seldom is any indication given of the complex business of growing up and if there ever were lazy bullies among the staff, you would never know.

In the case of Gwendraeth Grammar School, situated some three miles from Cefneithin, where Carwyn was to spend seven years after his local primary school, a handsome publication celebrating fifty years of the school's existence is a paean of praise for the old grammar school system.* Seeing it, I could not help comparing it with a similar publication of my own grammar school at Pontypridd which, although the school was much older, was nevertheless smaller and more dowdy, probably because it was printed when wartime restrictions reduced the amount of paper available. Immediately,

---

* ed. T. W. Pearce, *Gwendraeth*, Christopher Davies.

there are two sharp differences. The amount of material written in Welsh is markedly greater in the Gwendraeth souvenir while the war casualties amongst the old boys of Pontypridd Grammar School were almost ten times as many, a matter not just of numbers (Pontypridd was an all-boys school while Gwendraeth was mixed) but one more way in which the war and its casualties shadowed my schooldays.

My own memories as Carwyn's exact contemporary were of heartbreak and tragedy – there was hardly a street or a road in my neighbourhood untouched by such deaths, whereas Carwyn recalls just two boys killed, one of them the side-stepping outside-half of the village whom he was to remember on many occasions. It is probable that the exclusive concentration on two industries, mining and agriculture, both reserved occupations and exempt from call-up, accounted for this difference and, of course, there is a ready explanation for the number of articles and reminiscences written in Welsh, for Welsh was the language of the playground and much of the teaching.

Gwendraeth, like other such schools, was to play host to evacuees, one group from a London girls' school, another from heavily bombed Swansea, and military service meant that female members of staff were in the majority. As might be expected, the Headmaster, Mr Llewellyn Williams, became Commanding Officer of the Home Guard; the Air Training Corps held its meetings in the art room where German bombers were displayed for identification purposes; and once, on the occasion of the only air battle to be fought over Drefach, the Deputy Headmaster resorted to his cane to drive admiring and enthusiastic spectators into the safety of an improvised air-raid shelter. Once and only once was the legend 'exam interrupted by enemy bombing' written on examination papers.

Carwyn himself recorded a much more normal kind of harassment – his very first day was clouded by the fact that he stood out conspicuously since a friend of his mother's had knitted him a special pair of navy blue stockings with bright yellow tops, the subject of much caustic comment as they were immediately visible below his short trousers. Presumably they were the wrong colours. Then there were the usual minor tortures inflicted on new boys – some heads were ducked in the lavatory pans, some were sent on fool's errands to a local shop where cigarettes were obligingly sold singly – and no doubt the school buildings seemed vast, the assembled staff in their black gowns at first sight formidable and distant.

At the end of his first day, Carwyn's mother asked him, 'How did it go?'

His surly answer was (he records), 'No more of those bloody stockings for me!'

It is curious that in all the time I knew him I seldom heard him swear and yet this sentence written in the jubilee brochure and published in 1975 must have been inserted deliberately, probably because the school's most famous pupil (after Barry John and with yet another Welsh fly-half, Gareth Davies, waiting in the wings!) was suffering from a glut of admiration. What is clear is that he found at Gwendraeth an ideal world in which he soon became the ideal pupil, and it requires no act of the imagination to envisage the school career that was eventful only because it was almost completely without blemish. He was to become simply the kind of pupil for which the founders had strived, a template, a model, the mix of scholar, athlete and sportsman that puts the victor into *victor ludorum*! And he never ceased to be grateful.

He records exactly:

> Looking back over those years, the lingering impression I have is one of belonging to one happy family. The staff were counsellors and friends, skilful, patient and wise disciplinarians. I feel that the school reflected the local coal mining community with its intense respect for learning. A warm, close community where everyone knew everyone else. Snobbery was anathema to all, and anyone who tried it on, was soon cut down to size.

No school had better teachers. A united and willing staff does not happen by chance; there must always be a firm, unobtrusive hand at the helm, and this school certainly had. The respect felt and shown for Mr Llewellyn Williams by both staff and pupils was prodigious. He was a headmaster from the top of his head to the soles of his feet . . .

This is Carwyn giving references as glowing as the ones he was to receive himself. Propriety stalks the school corridors. It might seem too good to be true and, as with all grammar schools, there is never any hint of the elitism which subordinated two-thirds of the school to live in the shadow of the academic high-fliers. But in Carwyn's case it probably was true, for he was able to succeed at everything and nothing succeeds like success. His good luck was that he found an immediate rapport with his form mistress, Miss Beti Hughes, of whom he wrote, 'No pupil could have a gentler, kinder teacher to help in the transition to a strange new world' and as the first years went by, two other teachers, his Welsh mistress, Miss Dora Williams, and his sports master, Mr Gwynfil Rees, between them established the most rewarding patterns of his life. Indeed the praises, each of the other, teacher and pupil, the immaculate school reports and the glowing magazine paragraphs after the pupil had succeeded are like the reflections of lives in a Welsh fairy story, a simple, cautionary tale, in all a perfect description of how things should be – indeed all that educationists had always aspired to, totally in keeping with the noble hope quoted on the flyleaf of the jubilee brochure, the remarks of another distinguished old boy, a former director of education for Pembrokeshire, Mr Wynford Davies:

> When you leave school, you may well be scattered all over the country, indeed all over the face of the earth. But the school you will remember is that of your school

fellows and your teachers – how you got on together, what magic casements were open to you during your years in school, what games you played, what friendships you made, what hopes and aspirations you had – these things will be your school and you will remember it.

It is hard not to come to the conclusion that he was exactly right in Carwyn's case and while, to the sceptical observer like myself, there is an air of unreality about such hopes no suggestion of the possibility of beating or bullying or failure, or of the great unfairnesses of life – there was not the slightest evidence that Carwyn was ever aware of them at Gwendraeth because the school and its waiting avenues of success absorbed him totally and it is a fact that he never wrote about the school at all, except in testimonial English. I can remember vividly talking to him about some of the causes of truancy much later in life – we were by then both ex-schoolmasters – and I pointed out that one of the reasons why children invented excuses for staying at home was the fear that one of their parents might abscond, and cited an actual and extraordinary case where a poor boy driven mute with anxiety hung about his neighbourhood spying unseen upon his mother whom he feared might elope. Carwyn was appalled at such a thought and at times like this he displayed an unbelievable naivety.

Part of his lifelong objection to the comprehensive system was his belief in the corrupting effect on excellence of the great mass of humanity. In his mind, it was as if the borders were permanently drawn in childhood by the scholarship examination and he had little interest in the less able. In educational terms he was an elitist, and remained so.

As might be expected, he seems never to have experienced any serious difficulty in school as his reports show. The commendations fall like acorns after a storm and while there are a few promptings 'to try a little harder' or an occasional note of 'a lapse of concentration', it is hard to believe that he ever gave anyone a moment's concern. The only villain was sport: 'Carwyn has ability and his future career should be a very successful one, *provided he puts his work first.*'

Although he was to praise his English master, Mr Gwilym John Evans (whom he was to reward with his solitary distinction in English literature), it is clear that the two principal influences were Miss Dora Williams and Mr Gwynfil Rees. Miss Dora, as she is referred to constantly in the brochure by former pupils, was much praised as an inspired teacher of Welsh literature and of her, he was to write: 'I owe a great deal to Miss Dora, the gentlest of teachers and one possessed of a formidable intellect.' It was she who arranged for her pupils to hear the very first Welsh language broadcasts of the Welsh poet and scholar, T. H. Parry Williams, in a private house, and later she produced plays and stimulated the writing of poetry and short stories amongst her pupils. It was she who also introduced Carwyn to the Welsh poet Gwenallt who with T. H. Parry Williams became Carwyn's future tutors at Aberystwyth University, and later still his referees. If the strands of the major influences of his life could be laid out for dissection, there is no doubt Miss Dora would be one of the strongest sinews, and one that attached the past to the future.

Doubtless, she was first impressed by Carwyn's command of the Welsh language, and then, by introducing him to the poets and thinkers who came to be his favourites, she set the course which was to lead to his complete assurance of his nationality, the confidence and the never wavering belief in the idea of Welsh nationhood. She also provided him with the opportunity to perform in school eisteddfodau which he did frequently, and while others sometimes remember her as a fussy and rather severe spinster 'with no liking for rugby football!', her influence was frequently remarked upon by Carwyn who travelled to North Wales to see her in her retirement and had earlier been devoted to her during a period of her life when she was an invalid. He was never one to forget his mentors and perhaps a good part of her influence and that

of the poets she bade him read constantly is best explained by
the feeling of security they must have given him. Whereas the
teaching of Welsh was regarded by many in the East as an
irrelevance, Miss Dora encouraged Carwyn to probe more
deeply into the culture he was rooted in and made him at
home in Welsh literature. It was a natural progression from
the culture of his home, and beyond that the countryside of
which he wrote describing the period of his life before his
teens:

> I hate the sickly smell composed of new leather and the
> fumes of the Western Welsh bus, so welcome the break
> at Carmarthen and Pont Henllan to change buses. The
> rounded hills, the wooded slopes, and the placid,
> leisurely animals in the field are a joy, and to arrive in
> Rhydlewis, a little village in South Cardiganshire where
> my mother was born, is like entering the promised land.
> I always look forward to it so much, keeping awake at
> night as I used to on Christmas Eve and on the eve of
> the Sunday School trip, but those nocturnal journeys on
> which I travelled so hopefully were as nothing compared
> with the real experience.
>
> Here I am in Moelon, a dairy farm where everyone
> speaks nervously and quickly in my mother's Welsh and
> in Moelona's Welsh, so I feel at home as if it were
> *Nantoer*, a family novel which my mother was so proud
> to read to us during the long winter nights, before we
> had a radio, because she knew the author.
>
> I rush out to meet the cows and the calves, pretend to
> look at the bull because I'm afraid of him, ride on my
> uncle Tom's tractor, and savour the prospect of a month's
> holiday in the heart of South Cardiganshire away from
> the coal dust and the black pyramids of waste. I firmly
> decide not to be homesick.
>
> Before going to William Thomas's Y.M. to play ping-
> pong and snooker and renew friendships made over the
> years with Terwyn Maesyfelin, Dai Dolanog, Albie and

others, I call on Dan Teiliwr and Ianto Bach, still busily making suits, who tell me yet again about my grandfather whom I had never seen, a carpenter, a real craftsman and master builder, so they claim. Later they go into ecstasies over another forebear who apparently was a poet or, as I suspect, a versifier.

I know I belong, that my roots are here, and feel guilty that I am the only one of the family not born a Cardi, not born in Rhydlewis. Tonight, I am not just a small boy, but the romantic who has found his Ynys Afallon far away from the realities of life, the school, the black pyramids, the dread of the ambulance and the disturbing siren.

This is one of the last fragmentary glimpses of his schoolboy self. He never wrote or spoke about the kind of culture shock which a grammar school education (without Miss Dora) presented to other boys. Those who did not study Welsh writers could take a dip out of a celebrated volume, *More Essays By Modern Masters*, then an approved set book. It included the essays of Robert Lynd and A. A. Milne, one of which, 'Going Out To Dinner', was presented to schoolboys like Carwyn who would sometimes hurry home from school to meet their fathers and their workmates coming home black from the colliery. While the fathers bathed in the tin bath in front of the fire, there was required reading for the boys.

If you are one of those lucky people whose motor is not numbered (as mine is) 19 or 11 or 22, it does not really matter where your host for the evening prefers to live: Bayswater or Battersea or Blackheath – it is all the same to your chauffeur. But for those of us who have to fight for bus or train or taxicab, it is different We have to say to ourselves, 'Is it worth it?'

While the selection of such pieces for study now appals me because of their incongruity, Carwyn was eager to read as widely as he could. But Welsh literature was altogether more exciting.

By contrast, in the same years, the poet Gwenallt was to publish a famous essay which, like his poetry, spoke directly of the Welsh experience. Like Carwyn, Gwenallt had grown up in an industrial area, in his case Pontardawe in the Swansea Valley, but the original home of his family was in rural Carmarthenshire. He too had the same connection with older roots, spending the summer holidays with relatives on farms, and was brought up with the same values, values which were maintained through the chapel. This was the old Wales of the nineteenth century with its black and white values and long established non-conformist customs. 'The chapel where I go stands in an industrial village,' wrote Gwenallt. It might have been Carwyn himself.

> I went every Sunday to morning service; to Sunday School in the afternoon; to the five o'clock meeting, where the young were taught how to pray aloud in public; to the evening service; to singing practice; to the prayer meeting (the *seiat*) each week; to the dawn service on Christmas morning; to a whole week of prayer meetings in the first week of January; to sit examinations in the Scriptures; and in summer I would go on the Sunday School trip to the seaside.

Gwenallt also wrote of the life outside the home in Alltwen:

> I used to take lunch to my father in the steelworks. I remember the dusky yellow light inside the works, and the waves of heat that took the breath out of my nostrils and dried my throat up. I was allowed to go to the stage by the furnace where the furnacemen in blue goggles and with cheeks flushed red worked in their vests shovelling the scrap into the mouth of the furnace with long shovels. One of them would put the blue goggles on my eyes, and through them I would see the metal bubbling in a haze of white heat on the floor of the furnace. I would see the furnace being tapped, the molten metal

poured into the ladle in the pit, and then from the ladle into the moulds; and when it had solidified, the crane lifting the steel ingots and stacking them alongside the tramlines, I used to be frightened when I saw the ingot swinging from the hook on the crane above the workmen in the pit.*

It is not difficult to understand how Carwyn came to revere Gwenallt, nor indeed to understand his gratitude to the teacher who introduced him to such a writer. Miss Dora, of course, would have none of the snobbish indifference, if not the total ignorance of Welsh writers frequently found amongst teachers of English literature in Wales an ignorance that extended and extends to Welsh writers in both languages. The feeling, extraordinary to outsiders – if it's Welsh, it can't be much good! – is a part of the anglicised provincial intellectual's inferiority and remains lurking like a damp mist in a good deal of Welsh life, particularly in towns and cities. It was always a matter of astonishment to Carwyn who frequently discussed it. If he became one of the most confident Welshmen of his generation, it was because in his early years he had an education of which he could be proud.

Miss Dora was one of the first of those significant individuals who was to mould Carwyn's character outside his home. Her North Walian indifference to rugby football, the spinster cocking her nose at the religion of the riff-raff probably also appealed to him, for the idea of a riff-raff was always firmly implanted in his mind, especially where education was concerned.

The same Welsh gods of fortune who stood Miss Dora in Carwyn's path also took care that his sportsmaster, Mr Gwynfil Rees, was a graduate in Welsh from Aberystwyth University. He also knew both Gwenallt and T. H. Parry Williams and had been taught by them, and – to smooth the path even more thoroughly – was a children's author, a successful competitor

* transl. Andre Morgan and Ned Thomas, '*Credaf* (What I Believe)', *Planet* 32.

at local eisteddfodau, winner of minor bardic chairs, as well as being big enough, strong enough and footballer enough to have sent W. T. H. Davies flying in a charity rugby match, being a head-on tackler of note! It was as if these gods of fortune, meeting at some great Welsh county councillors' selection committee in the sky, deliberated long and hard to find even a sportsmaster whose cultural connections were impeccable. In retrospect, knowing how much Carwyn was revered all his life, particularly in West Wales, it is not difficult to imagine the councillors in debate overhead. Once convened, the celestial minutes come readily to hand.

'Item Four now, boys. Shortage of fly-halves. We've got young Carwyn James coming to Gwendraeth?'

'Hear hear!'

'No, no! We've got Miss Dora for the culture proper, the point now under discussion is who are we going to get for him in rugby?'

'What about so-and-so's nephew?'

'No, no! Not relatives this time. This is our Carwyn!'

'Very deserving case, my nephew . . .

'Can't help that. This is rugby. If we give him Miss Dora for the inside stuff, we've got to find somebody as good outside. Not a Physical Training Thick, I mean, to put it blunt.'

'What d'you mean, a P.T. Thick? I got relatives, P.T. Thicks, doing marvellous work all over the county!'

'Got to get someone who'll suit the boy. Now let's go through them one by one . . . How many BAs have we got on the books who can drop kick?'

In the person of Gwynfil Rees, the gods (and the celestial county councillors!) must have been united and no one who has met Gwynfil Rees could fail to realise that here was a man, a strong, genial and humorous presence to whom Carwyn would forever be drawn, and to whom, as a footballer, he would forever be indebted. Indeed, as in so many of the relationships which extended over Carwyn's life, there was a reciprocity which endured.

As it was, not a great deal of rugby was played at the school in the early years of the war. Carwyn says:

At the time I don't think that we were aware of the restrictions imposed by the war effort, we simply took it for granted that organised games could not be played. I spent many a pleasant afternoon playing soccer for the local youth club. My tenuous claim to fame during this period was an offer by a smooth-talking Cardiff City scout to take part in a soccer trial which I declined. (He was actually offered an apprenticeship.) When the Cefneithin ex-schoolboys' side began playing matches in the season 1945/6, I became a playing member, and I was barely sixteen when I played in my first cup final against Pen-y-banc at Llandybie.

He says in another article that when rugby was resumed at Gwendraeth, he played his first inter-school match as captain and fly-half, an indication of the effect of club football upon him. But in the years that followed, after the age of sixteen, the pattern of his Saturday life was to play for the school in the morning and village sides in the afternoon.

Gwynfil Rees remembers noticing his pupil first in the gymnasium as a natural athlete. In rugby he was a reluctant fingertip tackler until he was taken out specifically by his sportsmaster and made to tackle the burly school hooker who was constantly bidden to run at him, an unpleasant process of which Carwyn complained. But years later he took the trouble to send a cutting from the *Yorkshire Post*, describing 'a brilliant last-minute tackle by the Welsh Secondary Schools Captain' to his mentor. He had done the right thing at last! It was the same mentor who constantly complained about his predilection for dropping goals to whom he turned and gave a thumbs-up sign at Cardiff Arms Park after his one and only drop goal in a senior international against Australia in 1958. Drop goals won matches and Carwyn played to win. Gwynfil Rees also remembers that although Carwyn was expressly coached for the Welsh Secondary Schools XV, he was not at first selected whereupon he promptly wrote a poem to express his disappointment. Later he was to win six caps as a schoolboy, meeting another of his lifelong friends, Clem Thomas, who was his schoolboy captain in Paris in 1947. By the end of his school career, Carwyn had begun playing in senior football and was already a good cricketer, playing for Tumble where he is remembered dreamily making stylish strokes at the non-striking end of the wicket. He also broke the county record for throwing the cricket ball.

Although Carwyn blotted his copybook for the first and only time by failing geography in the Higher School Certificate Examination, the failure gave him the opportunity to stay on in school and become head prefect for the second year in succession, one indication of how highly he was regarded, but poor luck for some nameless boy who might have benefited his own career by being given the opportunity. The favourite remained favourite and does not seem to have caused many resentments.

His headmaster, Llewellyn Williams, who was also to remain a friend, wrote:

> He is the most able of the pupils who have passed through this school. Indeed, should the opportunity ever arise, I shall be pleased to offer him an appointment to my staff.

It was the ultimate praise (though the offer of a teaching post was not, alas, in his gift) and again it is not difficult to call up a picture of this head prefect, captain of rugby football, a schoolboy international, a good cricketer and athlete, ultimately gaining admission to a university that, as he says, simply had to be Aberystwyth University which housed as teachers the poets whom he read constantly.

At the same time, there was another side to his life, one that was equally important, for in his success in school he was probably not much different from those who succeeded at school all over the country. The confidence of the son of a Labour peer at Eton would not be very different if it were based on equal success at studies and in sport. It would also probably be matched by a general acceptance by those in power for it is unlikely that anyone succeeding even to schoolboy authority could hold many views unacceptable to the staff or headmaster. The head prefect would in all likelihood be an agreeable conformist and, if the sum of his life was his school career, lived intensely and swathed in the warm glow of adult approval, there is a danger that such a life ever after would be an anticlimax and a disappointment. Carwyn, I am sure, meant everything he said in praise of his school and they must have been among the happiest years of his life. He was not, however, exclusively immersed in them for his skills as a rugby player and a cricketer were of course known outside the school and in playing for Cefneithin and other neighbouring village sports teams, he was reuniting himself with his old primary school classmates.

The village, like all Welsh villages, had a character of its own, and the head prefect was unusual and untypical in that his sharp eye for a ball had led admirers to construct a small wooden stand to allow him an adult's reach on the snooker table in the village hall. In common with many South Wales boys, the billiard ball was another part of his education, an anteroom to the prefects' common room where the company of miners and their sons was a less rarified but a welcome addition to complete a young man's experience in what councillors of the day were pleased to call the school of life. The bard-to-be, the bachelor of arts, the Welsh scholar who introduced the restaurant to complaining rugby club treasurers also potted a wicked black on the snooker table, and there was nothing he liked better all his life than the comfortable smoke-ridden aroma of the billiard hall, the clicking of the balls and the shuffle of the metal pointer on the scoreboard providing the congenial atmosphere of one more home to him.

The billiard hall was one more place which brought him into close contact with his fellows, at the same time, one more chance to stand out above most of them in ability. It was this ability, a dexterity of hand, foot and eye (which was confined exclusively to sport for he could not thread a pyjama cord and screwdrivers recoiled from his hand), that made it natural that he should be sought after as a representative player. It led him into all kinds of company, creating aspects of his personality which sometimes seemed to slot into compartments, but which extended into every single institution of Welsh life. On the one hand, there was the interior Carwyn, the sensitive soul of the vignettes; on the other, the man of sporting skills, the deft, eager hands stretching confidently for bat, ball, or cue. There was also the head prefect and the *victor ludorum*, and then there was the very local boy, modest as ever, as well liked in the billiard saloon as the chapel – it is not difficult to imagine him as the leading light in chapel, fond eyes gazing upon him from every pew. Untypically he never seems to have been much interested in girls although he was spoken of with veneration, particularly by his headmaster's daughters. There can be few young men who succeeded in so many different activities, few so desirable, none so modest and, it seems, so lacking in noticeable aggression.

Things came easy to Carwyn, although after the vignettes describing his early school life, apart from his weekly articles for the *Guardian*, he never wrote at any length, never did complete the autobiography which he began several times with much good advice and encouragement from his friend John Reason of the *Sunday Telegraph*. Indeed, he never wrote any substantial book except in collaboration, and it was Barry John, the Wales and British Lions fly-half his one-time ball boy on the village field beyond the garden of Rose Villa, who jumped the gun in 1974. His autobiography, *The Barry John Story*, prompted Carwyn to try and fail himself once again.

Barry John, the conquering hero, began his tale with a splendid local tribute to Cefneithin and the principal influence upon his early rugby-playing career, his Uncle Lloyd.

I only wish that my Uncle Lloyd had lived to see me take that last record-breaking penalty kick at Cardiff Arms Park in front of that huge crowd!

Where Carwyn hesitated and failed, Barry John plunged in, relating his own career with relish. When Barry played for Gwendraeth Grammar School, he was asked to play illicitly for the Carmarthenshire Police Team in mid-week games, and on games afternoons he would disappear from the playing fields to meet Hubert Peel, Llanelli's trainer, who would be lying in wait on the road outside the school, the engine of a getaway car running. After the journey (presumably in a black sedan) Barry would play under an assumed name and in the dressing-room afterwards he watched with interest as the policemen held a collection, a hat being passed around 'for the Special Branch', those co-opted members working 'under cover'.

Carwyn, prompted by these titbits, had a flood of memories of the same Uncle Lloyd who had played a similar part in his own career. It was he who had commented caustically on Carwyn's decision to play for Amman United instead of the village team. This was after Carwyn had left for university, but he too had relished the illicit visit of a deputation of five Amman United officials who came to his house 'one dark evening to persuade me to play for the best and richest team in Wales!'

It was to cause endless speculation in the village. Were they Rugby League scouts? It also led to the famous taxi, and much later, after Carwyn had returned to play for Cefneithin, he demanded the same star treatment. But when Cefneithin were knocked out of the cup, Uncle Lloyd was the first to comment for all to hear, 'That's the last bloody taxi you'll have!'

Everyone in South Wales has met Uncle Lloyd and his type, the supporter and committeeman whose passion makes an afternoon on the terrace an alternative sport. Carwyn, too, was caught up with the spirit of the man. In an unpublished memoir, he wrote of Uncle Lloyd:

When he spoke his comments loudly, he knew no greys or half colours. Life to him was black or white. In this mood, a favourite remark was, 'No-bloody-compromise!' He thrived on argument, and there was no place better than a rugby ground for a rousing argument. He would throw his cap in the air, stamp on it, cover his eyes with it, merely to demonstrate to those around him his disgust at an injustice inflicted upon one of his players either by the opposition or by the referee. Invariably, there was someone of a similar temperament present ready to disagree and to argue, and whilst the game went on, Lloyd and his adversary would be quite oblivious to the proceedings, having more fun on their own.

At the same time, Carwyn in later life was plagued by enthusiastic supporters who bent his ear with the constant expression of their views. Of them he was to quote a satirical verse:

> The game? He hardly saw a move, but he shouted
>   with gusto,
> And read of it in full that night in the *Echo*.*

He also recorded the cloak-and-dagger aspect of Welsh rugby life as Barry John had done:

> How well do I remember a Sunday evening in January 1958 around 5 p.m. being summoned to Emlyn House and finding an excitable Lloyd hardly able to contain himself with the news that Cliff Morgan had cried off and that I had been selected to take his place against Australia on the following Saturday. For confirmation and further drama which Lloyd loved, I had to ring Ivor Jones a member of the Big Five – the selection committee.

---

* Twm Tebot.

That particular evening, before the first of Carwyn's two international caps was awarded, occurred much later. But like Barry
John, Carwyn was thoroughly caught-up in the village enthusiasms. There were, as ever in his life, hands beckoning,
calling him insistently, for he was always a wanted man. If he
was sometimes aloof, he was never precious and his upbringing was not sheltered in any way other than that he had
little experience of failure. He was the emerging local hero, it
is true, but there were, as far as rugby football was concerned,
several setbacks before he left the village for university.

> Before I left Gwendraeth I had already played a couple
> of matches for Llanelli RFC. The first in partnership with
> Handel Greville was against Bridgend at the Brewery
> Field, and the second was at Pontypool in opposition to
> two of the finest wing-forwards then playing, Alan
> Forward and Ray Cale. It speaks volumes for the lack
> of foresight of the club's twelve-man selection committee
> in the late 'forties that they should have given such a
> baptism to a seventeen-year-old. The following season I
> learned my lesson at the Gnoll in Neath in the form of a
> late tackle by a fourteen-stone centre which shattered my
> confidence and put a temporary end to my first-class
> career.

Barry John had a parallel experience which, as might be expected
for a future rugby king with a coronation every winter, ended
differently. He was made of smarter stuff.

> The police were playing Laugharne and my brother Del,
> a more experienced player than me, had warned, 'Stay
> home, Barry, it'll be damned rough.' He was right. I
> needed all my skill as an artful dodger. Soon after the
> match started, I fielded the ball and called out, 'Mark!'
> only to see the Laugharne full-back bearing down on me
> like a train and clearly unstoppable. No time to dodge.
> I raised my foot in self defence and he collapsed like a
> shot stag.

Barry John was playing, as he says, under a *nom-de-rugby*.

Had my name appeared in the papers I would have been
in trouble on two counts. I wasn't a member of the police
force and on three occasions I was a truant. So when
one of the officials submitted a report to the local newspaper, one of the other players took the credit for the
points I scored.

'C'est la guerre,' as they might have said in Cefneithin Workmen's Hall.

Gwendraeth Grammar School was also to have another
Welsh outside-half in the person of Gareth Davies (all three
first capped against Australian tourists) and, indeed, the jubilee
brochure contains a photograph of all nine of the school's
senior internationals. All are immaculately suited, unembarrassed and gazing at the world with the expected aplomb.
Indeed, there is an air of chapel propriety about them, as befits
their status in life. The former head prefect gazes quizzically
into camera while his protégé, Barry John, as might be
expected, has an altogether more mischievous grin and wears
the most elegant double-breasted suit. It is an imposing group,
a posed photograph taken of the school's élite in all their glory
and who would deny it them?

But for an act of fate, a quirk of fortune, perhaps a day off
for the celestial gods up above in their cloudy chamber,
Carwyn might have been standing in the middle of the group,
suitably gowned as headmaster with his arms folded as headmasters do. He had every qualification except the important
South Walian connection, a few earthy and very local councillors on his side. But this he had not and when the time came,
the qualifications of another candidate were preferred despite
his headmaster's open declaration in favour of his golden boy.
But that is a story for later.

Chapter Four

You're playing Saturday!

I once lent Carwyn Carlos Baker's biography of Ernest Hemingway, a massive and thoroughly researched volume by the Woodrow Wilson Professor of Literature at Princeton University who, in approved fashion, dedicated his book to his wife with an appropriate indication of his gratitude. She had, in his words, 'fought it out during a seven-year siege', the length of time taken to complete the volume. My original intention was to awaken Carwyn's interest in the American literature of which he was woefully ignorant, and also to draw his attention to the way Hemingway saw aspects of the Spanish character reflected in the bullfight for it was my belief that there were similar observations to be made and lessons to be learned about the way in which the Welsh played rugby football. Carwyn listened gravely, read through the book, finally returned it to me with an appalled look and a felt exclamation.

'Good God!' he said of the massive 702-page volume. 'He's catalogued every drink Hemingway ever took!'

It is a point, and in the writing of those aspects of Carwyn's life of which I have no direct experience, I have to accept the views and memories of those who knew him without making such a catalogue. Carwyn the Blameless, Carwyn the Head Prefect, became in Aberystwyth University a less easily categorised figure just as, at the end of his four years there, he disappeared unobtrusively into the Coder Branch of the Royal Navy for his period of National Service.

In Aberystwyth in 1948, he was among a minority of students who went to university straight from school for it was the age of the ex-serviceman, of older men who had returned from the war to begin or complete their studies, thus introducing a more robust atmosphere to the common rooms and lecture halls, perhaps a worldliness that would otherwise have been absent. In rugby terms, it was to provide many schoolboys with an unexpected additional education for the ex-servicemen were older, more weathered and physically matured.

Carwyn, fresh from the glories of being a Welsh Secondary Schools international with his few games for Llanelli, soon found himself a second fifteen player, being kept out of the college side by John Brace, brother of Onllwyn, a fly-half and captain, whose team place was never in doubt. It was even less in doubt when Carwyn failed to attend one of the first rugby trials because he was demonstrating against railway closures for Plaid Cymru at Tregaron on that particular afternoon. It was probably the first time that his beliefs were to interfere with his rugby ambitions.

Carwyn shared lodgings near the playing fields with ex-Gwendraeth pupils, the lodgings found appropriately through his chapel. In the years that followed he divided his time between his courses in Welsh history, literature and geography with appearances for the College Second XV and Aberystwyth Town, as well as occasional games at home when the taxi came to collect him. As in his later life, his days became compartmentalised. There was attendance at lectures and periods of study which he carried out conscientiously, there was membership of the debating society which met every Friday in the winter months, a well-attended social evening where, as the terms went by, he began occasionally to get to his feet, his speeches always associated with Welsh issues. This was the head prefect, Miss Dora's prize pupil, gently finding his feet in a world a little more sophisticated than the one he had left, but made all the more congenial by the presence of his favourite poets in the flesh. He also regularly attended the Celtic Society and was a member of Baker Street Congregationalist Chapel. As might be expected, he was a favourite of his landlady who, we can be sure, mothered her Gwendraeth charges, making their beds and introducing order to their domestic lives as completely as she could. He was happy, he was among friends, and the move from home seems to have set in motion the kind of gradual transformation that would have attracted such hearty approval from the founders of the university that it is not difficult to imagine them raising glasses (of non-alcoholic beverage) in salute. Decades before, poor country boys had arrived there carrying the means of subsistence for each term, perhaps a sack of potatoes or a side of bacon, soon to be made at home in a small seaside college raised on the contributions of poor people. There is little doubt that a boy of Carwyn's background would feel immediately at home and be free of the frontal conflict of the English class system which greeted other students on their journey to the older English universities, or, as happened to others at this time, in the service messes where the Welsh experience was a poor preparation for the alien attitudes of an officer class.

At Aberystwyth there was also Plaid Cymru, the Welsh Nationalist Party student group which greeted freshmen on their arrival and provided the opportunity for like to meet like in the most convivial circumstances, with frequent visits from regular speakers. Gwynfor Evans, Plaid's first MP, recalls being taken by Carwyn and his close friend, Dafydd Bowen, now a Professor of Welsh at the University, to their lodgings for an impromptu supper after he had addressed the nationalist group. He remembers Carwyn as a good conversationalist, exceptionally ebullient and jolly company. Plaid Cymru is said to have had the strongest political party group on the campus, some of its members then and later obtaining high office in the Labour Party at Westminster, experiencing the prudent change of heart which led to power and material reward. Carwyn was president of the Plaid group in 1951 and '52, always active and vigorous in its demonstrations – he naturally attended a sit-down protest objecting to a gunnery range at Trawsfynydd. His nationalist friends then and in later days always felt he could be counted on for support at such demonstrations. His year as president is remembered as successful: numerous new members were enrolled, Carwyn's rugby charisma probably attracting some less likely individuals to the group. But to his student friend, Dafydd Bowen, who was responsible for his own recruitment, he expressed his gratitude, 'I like your company because you don't know anything about rugby and can't impose on me.' It was a strangely prophetic sentence indicating a need that was to continue throughout his life. He was then, and always, a cultural nationalist, committed, personally indifferent to power, the essence of his nationalism being rooted in his love of literature and language, and a simple conviction that Wales was an entity and ought to have its own government. This was more dominant in his mind than any economic considerations and he seems to have swum in congenial company like a Welsh fish in Welsh waters without, we must suppose, an angler in sight.

And then there was rugby, and for a time at least, the joys of second-class rugby, entirely free of the fierce competitiveness which later came to be the inevitable hallmark of the milieu in which he so distinguished himself as player and coach. It was an undemanding period of his life and at first he spent more time with his rugby friends than with any other group. Of this period, he wrote:

> We were a cliquish lot, we drank coffee together every morning in the refectory, we talked rugby between lectures, we took over the Ship for our after-match sing-songs.

He never describes these singsongs, but he is detectable in other people's reminiscences, sitting small and neat in his Welsh Schools XV blazer with its gold Prince of Wales's feathers before a modest and solitary brown ale while the foulest songs were sometimes sung by ex-servicemen whose wartime repertoire has seldom been equalled and frequently featured raucous descriptions of portions of King Farouk's anatomy and the state of his Egyptian harem. These sex-starved soldiers' songs gave a new dimension to bawdiness. But as the night wore on and the singers wore out, Carwyn's turn would come, a time for sentiment, and in the sweetest of light tenor voices he would sing the Welsh love song *Myfanwy*, hands crossed in his deacon's pose, bringing a reminder of the years of innocence which he was to carry with him all his life. This was the chapel Carwyn, carrying the pulpit in his voice, often changing the mood of the assembled company until hymns followed, very probably sending the singers home with a beery glow of maudlin satisfaction at this raising of tone before 'time' was called by the indispensable Treorchy landlord.

That Carwyn was fastidious, drank very little and kept his distance made no difference. It was the singer, not the song. The golden boy had produced a golden voice and it was to be put to good effect in another capacity in his fourth year when, as Captain of the First XV, he was required to be their advocate after the new vice principal, a woman, had decided on 'a little tightening of discipline'. It seems they had been guilty of the kind of behaviour which gave the rugby team a bad reputation. When the team played away, it stayed away and 'came back with the milk', and on occasion the stuffed heads of wild animals tended to disappear from public houses en route. The vice principal, Dr Lily Newton, stipulated after one such occasion that the team must be back in Aberystwyth by midnight. Soon afterwards the team left for a fixture at Birmingham University and in the absence of their captain (who was injured) did not return until 5 a.m. when it made its presence noisily felt. The captain was summoned and, although not personally involved, held responsible. It was a confrontation which is not hard to imagine and those involved feared the direst consequences, perhaps the prohibition of away games, a firm and understandable act on the part of a new vice principal determined to impose a more stringent rule now that most of the ex-servicemen had left. But Carwyn, made completely innocent by his own absence, emerged from the interview an hour later as silent victor and no restrictions of any kind were placed upon his team. No one knew exactly what he said, but he relates once again in his testimonial English that he first asked for understanding. He was, he said, most distressed by this unforgivable affront to the vice principal's rule. It would not have happened if . . . but then, just as she had problems, so did he. And so on. And all in the 'Myfanwy' voice with hands folded, the appeal overwhelming, including his sympathetic understanding of *her* problems. Later, omitting the details of his own appeal, he wrote, 'Dr Newton was most understanding of the problems facing the Captain of the wild young men of the rugby club used to the freedom given them *because of the presence of the ex-servicemen.*' It would all have been different if it had been left to Dr Newton and himself, of course; and if Hitler had not marched through Europe with the ultimate intention of alienating Welsh chapel boys from their Welsh roots, violating the countryside, corrupting ancient values etc. etc., all would have been different. But as it was, how could the captain help the vice president with *her* problems *in the future*?

It was Carwyn's first experience in the role of successful rugby advocate and it is doubtful if he ever won a more difficult case. There were no repercussions and his one line testimonial to the vice principal was duly written, although never published. All his life, he was better with mothers than their daughters and he can seldom have melted a harder heart to better effect. The game, he might have said, and as the Welsh Rugby Union insist, must go on. And it did.

There is another less known but important facet of Carwyn's life at Aberystwyth at which young rugby players today might look with envy. No one familiar with the contemporary Welsh club scene who has seen players lose form as game follows game for the full length of a gruelling season can but wonder at the obsession of officials with the weekly circus, all to the detriment of the poor horses. It is as if you feel at times, the treasurer rules and it is only by an act of transitory kindness, a sudden moment of compassion, that injured players are not required to shift the fruit machines from one floor of the club to another by way of recompense for the loss of their playing time, a token form of apology for any possible reduction in revenue at the turnstiles. Then there is the press, eager to promote, quicker to criticise, easily able to forget who, following the fever, keeps the spotlight turning as they look for the new star. In all the heat, the cauldron boils from September to April, simmering away like a rusting and blackened stew pot on the stove of a poor family whose only sustenance becomes congealed in a morass of overcooked vegetables, the ingredients diminishing in nutritious value as the weeks go wearily by.

The end result is that effectiveness has replaced grace and invention. Daring and ingenuity and genuine creativity are all as rare as fresh meat in a medieval winter's menu. Discerning supporters (small time financiers all) can look in vain for the breeding grounds of old, those lazy tributaries away from the main stream where the coaches do not thrash the water and young players can laze and please themselves about their rugby, and where, on rare occasions and in special circumstances, there is perhaps the odd award for the player who does not turn up, who has an agreeable excuse, say, the way a lock of hair falls over a young girl's brow, or perhaps the single showing of a rare film on a rainy Saturday afternoon, all significant evidence of some extra-territorial normality! It was, as it happens, in such circumstances at Aberystwyth that Carwyn played his best rugby according to his friends, finding in that congenial atmosphere (and, importantly, a wide pitch) the time and freedom from pressures to enjoy himself.

Certain individuals have special memories of unimportant games where Carwyn etched a place for himself in their minds as the fly-half of fly-halves, suddenly breaking down the middle,

creating havoc in crowded situations, a will-o'-the-wisp, here
and there and gone! And there is one particular memory of a
lovely April evening in a small valley tournament, with the
sun casting shadows as he broke clear in a seven-a-side game,
hotly pursued by a solitary wing whom he allowed to come
close, then accelerated, then slowed again, then sidestepped
on his enemy's shadow, dancing away, playing torero with his
heels until his pursuer finally fell sprawling, hands grasping
the air. Carwyn was to do this again and again, once, later, for
the London Welsh in the Middlesex Sevens when actually over
the line, wishing to touch down under the posts, he picked off
opponents and sidestepped past them one by one, a touch of
bravado, a look-no-hands! insolence all indicative of total
confidence from a fly-half who stood back on his heels and let
the ball come to him.

Those who speak of him, point to Barry John as the successor
most like him, but in his day contrasting styles were in greater
evidence: Cliff Morgan and Glyn Davies, who both ran on to
the ball, taking it on the burst, were in some ways more spec-
tacular. It was, and is, of course, an idle comparison since there
is all the difference in the world between first – and second-
class games, and both Davies and Morgan at the same age
played in different leagues for most of the time, being under
more pressure for longer periods when playing for first-class
clubs. But it is also probable that Carwyn, in a less pressurised
atmosphere, learnt the extent of what a fly-half could do and
went to the limits in discovering what he could do himself as
a player. As we observed Cliff Morgan's bunny-hugging run,
his head thrown back, veins showing as he made the outside
break, always under pressure and usually displaying a range
of facial expressions that belonged on the stage at La Scala,
especially when late-tackled, there could be no real doubt that
he was a more effective player who proved himself week after
week. But then Carwyn's spell in quieter waters undoubtedly
taught him much that was later to be of value to him as a
coach, and those who saw him play regularly and played

with him have special memories of his style, his immaculate kicking and the safety of those long tapering fingers above all, the grace of his movements and his willingness to take risks.

This is the kind of rugby memory that seems to be confined to his own generation. It is doubtful nowadays that you could even complete such a reminiscence without being shouted down by the terrace debaters who would pronounce that this was virtually unopposed rugby. That is not the point. It might have been an easier game, but it produced thought, elegance and style, and it was also characterised by that long forgotten ingredient, the intense enjoyment of the player and no thought at all of prestige, the name-and-fame aspect of rugby football which today tends to be the harsh bit between the teeth of the jerseyed horses. It is a point not to be exaggerated, and is in no way a detraction of the merits of his more successful rivals. Would that we had Glyn Davies, Cliff Morgan and Carwyn James to argue about next Saturday! But it was a golden time for Carwyn and the pleasures he derived then were always a part of him, the confidence and the knowledge of possibilities which became an essential part of his thinking as a coach.

Journalist, critic, broadcaster, he had done it all himself, somewhere or other, on this ground or that, and it was his unique credential. No one who regularly followed his Friday *Guardian* column could but realise that here was a man with a special view of rugby football, aware of all its possibilities, not so much a rebel as a classicist who had a memory of old, forgotten glorious ways, who could write: 'Rugby Football should be played like living a life: fury and fun, chivalry and enjoyment – and be for a shorter length of time than, in some moments, you'd like it to last.'

He also developed a philosophy that dates from his Aberystwyth days, that marks his debt to them and to the schoolboy football earlier in which he played his first inter-school game ever – as you might expect – as captain!

The boring coach will continually preach that mistakes must be cut to a minimum. The creative coach, on the other hand, will invite his players to go out there and make mistakes. They will achieve little unless they make mistakes. We must introduce a spirit of adventure. I loved the Lewis Jones approach – 'I may concede two tries but I'll score four!'

In Aberystwyth, it is probable that Carwyn himself developed, perhaps defined unwittingly for himself the qualities he was to ascribe to his most famous Welsh Lions, Barry John and Gerald Davies. 'I love an inner calm, a coolness, a detachment; a brilliance and insouciance which is devastating. Some sniff the wind – they created it.'

What is certain is that his own rugby persona was formed first at Gwendraeth, then at Aberystwyth, with a little tempering of the steel after his rides in the famous taxi to Amman United and Cefneithin – and all of it without a coach of any kind in sight! Indeed, in one of the many conversations I had with him about schoolboy football, his most treasured recollection was that of the old grammar school days when you might get the classics master on the duty roster to accompany the school team on away games. It made a nice change in the conversation, he said. It was the experts and the wise men, after all, who later picked this fly-half at centre for Wales!

Carwyn left Aberystwyth University in July 1952 with glowing testimonials from his mentors, having pursued courses in Welsh language and literature and been awarded an upper second class honours degree. No one would have been surprised if he had obtained a first, but there is a whisper of a panic in a Breton/Cornish paper, perhaps some unexpected texts, a surprise move by the examining body which denied him the highest honours. He had also completed a year's course of teacher training and had held office on the students' representative council. He was looked at in every way as the complete student. Outside the lecture hall, as ever in his life as a rugby player and a cricketer, he had already proved himself to be exceptional and his reputation went before him. He was sharp, he was alert, he was already being compared to W. T. H. Davies, the pre-war Welsh fly-half whose graceful running and stylish ways had been seen once more in Wales when Rugby League players were allowed to return to the Union game during the war.

Always in Carwyn's life there were the two continuing strands, the warmth with which he was regarded by his academic mentors, and which he in turn reciprocated, and then the sharp light of a brilliant rugby promise which shone about him, attracting others and making him just a cut above his fellows for no one in Wales is more special than a rugby player of such note. East Wales might yawn or look with blank incredulity at the prospective bard, but a prospective Welsh international fly-half was a modern Glyndŵr, a likely prince of an ungovernable realm who might even cause a Marxist finger to rise to the forelock – let county councillors tremble if they dare offend such a man (well, let them be warned anyway!). Such a player was welcome everywhere, and no doubt it was at this time that the name C. R. James – few could pronounce or spell Carwyn – was pencilled into a certain ledger at Oldham Rugby League Club. They and their kind had done well out of the Welsh clubs. But the enquiries did not end there, and the gentlemen of the rugby freemasonry had already begun to unwrap new aprons further afield.

In 1952, the Royal Navy had established itself as a rugby football service, and players like Malcolm Thomas and Bill Glastonbury, Welsh schoolmasters who had distinguished themselves playing for Devonport Services and the Royal Navy, had established a strong tradition. (Unlike myself whose twice-broken nose and semi-permanent concussion led only to a Certificate of Wounds and Hurts, gravely presented by the Lords Commissioners of the Admiralty, with a brief citation, 'Did fracture nasal bone while falling at the feet of forwards!') Such recruits, of course, would not be expected to go to sea, but there was a welcome for them and by this time it is probable that Admiralty moles were implanted throughout the land, especially in Wales where such matters could be quietly explained. Thus Gwyn Walters of Gowerton, a famous international referee, makes his appearance in Carwyn's life, just as he was later to perform a national service all on his own in Barry John's life, and Barry took care to record it. Mr Walters, then an area manager for the Forward Trust Finance House, saw an unemployed Barry John on BBC Television's *Sportsnight*, a congenial 'Situation Wanted' advertisement for a recently returned British Lion, and, being a financier and a referee, probably saw too the gold-tipped fountain pen glistening in a grasping St Helen's Rugby League hand. Very smartly he turned himself into an employment placement officer, directing the most gifted feet in the dole queue to more promising things.

In Carwyn's case, Mr Walters, as Carwyn relates, 'had an arrangement to divert promising players' to an unnamed naval officer in Devonport. It was a diversion which no one regretted and very soon afterwards, Coder (Special) James, D/MX 918946, marched through the gates of Victoria Barracks, Portsmouth, for a brief period of basic training which would eventually lead to an intensive Russian language course, the Cold War being at its height and a sudden need for Russian interpreters and translators being impressed upon all the three services. As an honours graduate he was a natural recruit, but as a rugby player with a proved potential which was known even before he put a foot on the barrack square, he was more than naturally welcome and was selected to play for Portsmouth's Combined Services team even before his marching boots were broken in. And even when they were, his instructors knew him first and foremost as a player of note. Once again this was a young man who was special and about him there was an aura.

There now began a period of his life which friends many years afterwards could not imagine: Carwyn on the barrack square, Carwyn sewing his name-tabs onto his socks, Carwyn confronted with spit and polish, actually falling in and falling out, performing movements with a rifle by rote. And his friends simply could not believe it ever happened. They did not know him, however, for he is reported to have mustered himself on time, to have been in all respects unobtrusive, even to have pulled a naval whaler around HMS *Victory*, and once in a long conversation, to have confessed to a friend that he would much prefer to abandon the intensive Russian course and all its academic chores which lay ahead 'to do more naval things!' He probably changed his mind soon afterwards for, following the initial training, he was drafted from the Combined Services XV to Devonport Services XV and on to a Signals School at Saltash where parade ground marching was now carried out with the use of signal flags, flag hoists which indicated a turn to port or starboard, and here Coder James had some difficulty. 'You wouldn't have thought, seeing him march, that he could move on the rugby field the way he did,' is a reasoned and polite comment. But since the coding procedures were largely an intellectual activity, he passed with ease, made his number with Devonport Services, and then passed on to the army camp at Coulsdon in Surrey, the Joint Services School for Linguists where naval and RAF personnel were guests of the army with a regimental sergeant major to contend with, for-midable tests in Russian every six weeks, and almost every night spoken for because of the intensity of the course. If Coder James was harbouring any apprehension on the journey from Devonport, it is likely it vanished from the moment he marched into the gates with the naval squad. Just as they were about to pass the guardhouse, an army squad bore down upon them – the two squads, one in blue, the other khaki, marching to attention and coming within feet of each other. Coder James was in the front rank, swinging his arms, but as he looked across the impassive face of an army lance corporal, eyes staring ahead, mouthed a singular greeting in the prisoner's lip language, 'You're playing Saturday!' The lance corporal was Cenydd Thomas, himself later a well-known international referee, and, as if to make the welcome even warmer, a postcard was awaiting Coder James at the naval quarters as soon as he had fallen out. It was from the London Welsh Rugby Football Club, one of whose officials happened to live nearby, and it wasn't long before Carwyn learned that Ken Rees, the Captain of the London Welsh, was also stationed nearby as an RAF officer. He was more than willing to call for his new recruit and offer him a lift to London, and no doubt presented a prestigious figure at the main guard gate.

Of this time, Carwyn wrote,

> I hated the whole idea of being in a military establishment, I resented having to do National Service, and having taken an honours degree, I found five hours of Russian per day, plus an inordinate amount of preparation in the evenings, tiresome.

Conditions in the camp were bleak that first winter. It was cold, there was a shortage of coke for the hut stove, and blankets were thought to be in short supply by Coder James and one or two of his contemporaries. In the camp cinema, an improvised hut, other blankets with specially tapered corners were draped along the walls to create better acoustics, but some evenings ratings took extra blankets in with them to watch the endless procession of Russian films. The smartest ratings, like Coder James, soon started going in without a blanket and leaving with one, their tapered telltale ends suitably tucked away.

With the threat of being relegated to the course below, the pressure of work was intensive and unrelenting and there was always a regimental sergeant major growling about the square. Clearly unimpressed by the rugby aura, he actually had the impertinence on one occasion to inform Coder James that his collar would have been a disgrace on the neck of a dog, a remark over which Carwyn brooded, but he wisely changed his collar and later gave impromptu imitations of the RSM in the safety of the hut. Carwyn, like others, was critical of the White Russian teachers, all refugees from Stalin, most of whom had no training in instructional techniques, but he soldiered on. There were Welsh friends in the naval contingent and as he got to know them the patterns of later life emerged. There was a Swansea coder whose brilliantly polished boots were made available to Coder James on the rare occasions when he found himself on guard duties, and one can image Carwyn thoughtfully poised before his friend's bunk watching as the boots were spit-polished and boned on the bunk opposite, always a laborious business. No one in the naval hut spoke Welsh, but there were army acquaintances whom he saw occasionally in the NAAFI who did, one of whom was later to become Controller of BBC Wales. For the moment, however, in the confines of his own hut, Carwyn had more pressing needs and, as the boots attained their supreme gloss on the bed opposite, he took a fatherly interest in them, expressing a proprietorial interest. 'Look after those boots, Les' – I need them Friday!' Haircuts were Pontypridd-inspired by another friend who manipulated a pair of ladies' armpit clippers to cut hair to a just-appropriate length. 'Not too close, Malcolm, I'm playing against France on Saturday.' Carwyn's friends, of course, were from all four corners of the British Isles and he was often reunited with them in later life, though his intimate and involuntarily recruited private staff tended on the whole to come from the rugby milieu. As always, he found friends everywhere, and attended a Congregationalist chapel in Coulsdon when he could. He even managed to escape the RSM's notice except for one further occasion when dirty brass buckles on his satchel cost him a weekend's leave, lost the London Welsh their fly-half and gave *The South Wales Echo* its first Carwyn James press story – 'Dirty Buttons Stop Coder James'. As it happened, a Welsh selector had travelled up to see that particular game but, as Carwyn wrote sardonically, 'He lost the chance to play *Opportunity Knocks* and discover me!'

During this time, Carwyn played a season for the London

Welsh, appeared for them in seven-a-side tournaments, and very soon found himself taking part in a trial for the Royal Navy team, first as a full-back. In the trial, knowing he would not be in contention unless he displaced the regular full-back who was also the captain, he lived dangerously, attacked continuously and dropped three goals to cause the sole selector, Captain H. C. Browne, CBE, DSO, RN to write him a letter after he was inevitably picked and gained his Navy place. Captain Browne, whose monocled figure later caused French players considerable amusement when the Navy toured France, was another figure mimicked by Carwyn and he never forgot the opening sentence of the letter, obviously provoked by his flashy performance in the trial.

> Dear James,
> There are three things I want you to do on Saturday. Number One – tackle! Number Two – tackle! Number Three – tackle!

He was also surprised, while playing at his normal position of fly-half for Devonport Services, when he was courteously thanked by the pack leader for finding touch. He later wrote, 'At home in Llanelli you only heard the voice of the pack leader when you missed a touch kick. You did not miss a second time.' It was, he said, the difference between English and Welsh rugby. But he could be the RSM himself on the field. The camp had a Linguists' XV of their own, and when the Welsh Guards came back to Caterham from the British Army of the Rhine, they at first refused a fixture to the mixed Linguists' group who were not eligible to play in the Army Cup. By this time Carwyn was captain, and when eventually a fixture was granted and the entire Guards Batallion were marched out to line the touchlines, their officers comfortably seated on their shooting sticks, Carwyn led his Linguists onto the field. Within minutes, after the first scrum, there was a singular commanding general's voice coming from the fly-half who was clearly unimpressed. It was a command that is remembered to this day by those who heard it:

> I want the ball *very* quickly because we're going to hit this lot *hard* from the start!

Whereupon he promptly dropped a goal to lead his side as they inflicted a heavy defeat, the elegance of the shooting sticks and their owners notwithstanding. In later games, he became very heavily marked and firmly ordered his scrum-halves to gather bruises and stitches rather than receive unwanted balls himself, later inspecting their battered faces and bloodied hands with an apologetic grin. 'We won though, didn't we?' The familiar patterns of his life were already obvious. Mild, inoffensive and impish off the field, his authority upon it was total. When he relaxed now, *Myfanwy* was replaced by a sweet Russian folk song which he sang, once backed by the camp's Russian choir in a concert, a haunting solo which struck at many hearts in a smoke-filled hut full of silent, thoughtful men: '*I remember, I remember, the things my mother told me.*'

Coder (Special) James eventually became Leading Coder James and took his demobilisation proficient in all respects. Those who knew him thought him sharp, quick, intelligent. He had no enemies and he complemented the company he kept, brought kudos to all on the sporting field, at rugby and cricket, and even did his damnedest to contribute to his hut's successful marathon effort to outshine the other services in a spick-and-span inter-service competition for the cleanest hut. 'The Navy has got to win, chaps!' Aided by Coder James who was a team man, the Navy did.

In later life, Carwyn very seldom referred to this period, although he occasionally greeted the Controller of BBC Wales in Russian, and few knew that he had served briefly on a naval patrol boat operating out of Hamburg. No sooner had he arrived home than the sentence which greeted him on his arrival at Coulsdon was repeated – 'You're playing Saturday!'

Now Swansea were about to tour Rumania and wanted him to travel. Still bound by the Official Secrets Act, he had first to obtain the permission of the Admiralty. It was given, although he spoke no Russian for most of the tour, probably under instructions, until he finally became so exasperated at the difficulties of communicating with a Czech soccer team that he addressed them and their female interpreter at length. It brought an immediate response from the interpreter who went out and brought him a Russian copy of Lermontov's poem, 'I touch your hand', which he always treasured. On this tour, he was also asked to sidestep before a cine camera and made the acquaintance of the intensive Russian training methods used by the Rumanians. He also records that sports medicine, then in its infancy in Britain, was well advanced in Rumania: a team of doctors examined the Swansea party, finding them unfit by home standards, even diagnosing what was to be a fatal heart condition in one of the players who until that moment had been unaware of it. The absolute concentration of the Rumanian governing body impressed Carwyn, but if he took anything away with him, it was the principle of skill transference from one ball game to another, and that was all. It was 1954, he was now twenty-five, nearly half his life was over. Wales beckoned. It was time to get back to the familiar things.

Family group, 1945.
The family portrait was insisted upon by Mrs James as Dewi, her eldest son,
was about to join the Royal Navy. Michael and Anne James (*seated*);
(*l to r*) Eilonwy, Dewi, Carwyn and Gwen.

Gwynant, the village store at Rhydlewis, Cardiganshire, 1925.
Carwyn was the only member of his family not to be born in Rhydlewis
which represented for him a kind of Avalon. Had he been born there,
he might not, he once said, 'have been doomed to play rugby'.

Mr James astride Genko at Rhydlewis.

Carwyn's sister Gwen,
a nurse in Gloucester.

Carwyn aged five.

The fly-half at play.
As a university player, Carwyn went to the limits in showing what a fly-half could do. 'He sidestepped on shadows and played torero with his heels, the most graceful of players.'

Miss Dora Williams, his Welsh teacher, who introduced him to the poets who later became his tutors at university, and later still his referees.

Gwynfil Rees, sports master at Gwendraeth Grammar School, 1945. He made Carwyn tackle, threatened to drop him from the school side if he continued to drop goals. When his protégé won the first of his two caps against Australia in 1958 and dropped a goal, he raised his hand triumphantly to his mentor in the stand.

The Student, Aberystwyth, 1950.
He charmed the vice principal when she threatened to cancel the rugby team's away fixtures after misbehaviour, but missed the first fifteen trial match, attending a political demonstration instead.

The Skipper.

left   As captain of the Welsh Secondary Schools XV with the captain of the French team, 1948.

top right   Carwyn as captain of the London Welsh seven-a-side team. They were winners of the Middlesex Sevens in 1954.

bottom right   Carwyn played his first match for Gwendraeth Grammar School as captain, where he instructed some of the masters on the rules.

The programme of a village concert for the Welsh Secondary Schools International, 1948. 'All proceeds will be presented to Caerwen James' – his name was frequently spelt wrongly, even in Cefneithin. Earlier, the colliers of Tumble had a spontaneous collection after he had scored his first century playing cricket for the village.

A Russian language tutorial group at the Joint School for Linguists, Coulsdon, 1952. Coder (Special) James is seated on the left. He sang in Russian at the camp concert, played for the Royal Navy, Devonport Services and the London Welsh during this period and later had to obtain Admiralty permission to tour with Swansea behind the Iron Curtain.

At the flat at the Via I Monti in Rovigo, Italy.
The world's greatest rugby coach and his literary pin-ups, the Welsh writers
and nationalist activists, Saunders Lewis, Kate Roberts, Gwenallt,
and the Welsh opera singers, Gwyneth Jones and Olwen Rees.

With Alun Richards at a village rugby club near Rovigo. In his weekly column for the local newspaper, Carwyn quoted Milton: 'Who overcomes by force hath overcome but half his foe'. The Italians asked, 'Was Signor James talking about forwards or backs?'

Carwyn with Barry John, his one-time village ball boy and later his British Lions star. Carwyn can be said to have introduced the first-class restaurant into rugby football tactics. 'He was a player's man and a treasurer's nightmare!'

The Tongans being taught to scrummage Carwyn's way.

The Happy Man.
Carwyn being interviews after
the Llanelli-New Zealand
match in 1972.

The Loner.
Many saw him as a lonely
man, often aloof. He was
unclubbable, never a
vote-getter, and would
not 'run for office'.
'He lived and died by his
own ability and would
not tout for favours.'

The Royal National Eisteddfod, Haverfordwest, 1972.

left Carwyn being admitted to the Gorsedd of Bards.

As President of the Day, Carwyn attacked MPs who changed
their political colours 'like animals their coats every winter'
and suggested that directors of education who neglected
their Welsh past 'should blush'.

Carwyn in top hat.
As a nationalist, Carwyn refused an MBE after the successful Lions tour of New Zealand in 1971 but he was an aristocratic figure in many ways and once confessed to a friend, the poet Dafydd Rowlands, 'I should have been born a count!' At the same time, few people called him 'Mister'. He was simply Carwyn to multitudes.

Carwyn and the Pope.
When his Rovigo team won the Italian championship, they were presented to
the Pope who said to Carwyn, 'They tell me it's a very rough game?'
He replied, 'Not if it's played properly.'

Carwyn with his
parents in 1971 outside
the new bungalow
which the children
provided for them.
Michael James lived
until he was eight-one,
thankful that his late
entry (at thirty) into
the colliery prevented
him from being fully
disabled by silicosis.
He outlived many of
his contemporaries,
some of whom died
in their forties.

Carwyn commentated on snooker for BBC Wales TV and was well able to hold
his own with most players. Whatever the game, he was a tactician,
his credo simply expressed – 'Get the basics right.'

Carwyn in reflective mood.

Chapter Five

Bell, Book and Nicotine

A man, having turned his half-century, sees pretty clearly,
*The people and the places which have moulded his life.**

Gwenallt's lines offer a place to pause at this halfway mark in
Carwyn's life. At twenty-five, it is clear that he had not the
slightest doubt that he would return to Wales, that his future
was inevitably bound up with the country of his birth. Others
to whom National Service opened up different horizons found
their characters slightly changed and some began to look
forward to another kind of life, becoming more ambitious,
often leaving Wales for ever. Some were placed under pressures
more subtle than the strict academic disciplines which seemed
to prevail at the school for linguists which was in some ways
but a rougher version of university life. Those young men
whose intelligence and aptitude were seized upon by the
services and selected for leadership positions, commissions or
senior non-commissioned rank, often found themselves weaned
away from ancient loyalties.

South Wales is a less class-ridden society than those areas
of England from which most National Service officers were
recruited. Anyone who has experienced the uniquely democratic
valley society, the chapel, billiard hall, grammar school mix
with its rugby club orientation will know the apprehensive
feeling of entering a naval wardroom or army mess where

---

* transl. R. Gerallt-Jones, *'Y Meirwon'* ('The Dead') from *Poetry of Wales*
1930-1970, Gomer Press, 1974.

accents and attitudes are sharply different. There is the problem of servants, knives and forks, social mores of a very strange kind, to say nothing of the occasional passed-over senior officer whose inflamed eyes and haughty demeanour present the young recruit with the dismaying feeling of having gone to the zoo as a visitor, only to find oneself in the cage with the oldest and most unwanted inhabitant.

In the presence of such creatures, who thirty years ago so often mouthed platitudes about the Empire, the South Walian can but rebel. They can be avoided, however, and to an immensely desirable, rugby-playing South Walian, the pressures are less drastic than those which face ordinary mortals. At the time, it was a common practice of my generation to study these returned heroes, a few years older than ourselves, with hawkish interest, often playing against them in old boys' matches where the immaculate tunics and Sam Brownes would hang on the dressing-room wall alongside our own shabby utility clothing. We were hypersensitive to the slightest change. By joining *them*, did they in any way reject *us*? The most common change was in the accent, and it was regarded as the first sign of abandonment if the young subaltern on leave displayed the slightest sign of the class-ridden voices expressing themselves in the approved tones known later as 'good power of command!' Those who did so inevitably seemed to leave Wales – such airs and graces could not be tolerated in the welfare hall or the rugby club where a healthy derision was ever present. There were also, of course, those who tried and failed, providing us with a source of rich jokes.

It should also be remembered that most of those who were just too young to go to the war viewed it nevertheless with enthusiasm, despite the casualties, since most of us, including Carwyn, were caught up by the intensive propaganda. The war and the beckoning world of the services offered clear advantages to individuals who had fallen behind in their studies, or who were not obvious high-flyers: there was a sudden reduction in alarm about the future. Where in 1938

an open scholarship to Oxford would send grammar school
headmasters into frothing ecstasies on the assembly hall platform as they called for the cheers of oafs destined at best for a
counter job at the GPO – cheers they guaranteed with
a mandatory half holiday! – by 1943, it was clear to those
approaching call-up age that the swots' day was almost done.
Did we not have the evidence of our own eyes, the sight of
those layabouts a few years ahead, hefty enough to shove in
the scrum, sitting their Central Welsh Board School Certificate
year after year until some of them even began to wear plus-
fours in Form Five? Did we not now see them return heavy
with rank, redolent of privilege, with first-class rail tickets and
casual mention of batmen? There was another life beckoning,
lurid tales of sexual conquest, all a sight more attractive than
the advanced Latin declensions of Form Six.

And when the boys came home there were reunions, usually
on the occasion of old boys' dances held in the school hall,
when uniforms were omnipresent. One such took place on the
steps of my own school outside a newly built block when two
former classmates met after an absence of three years which
had sent one to sea as a humble but much torpedoed merchant
seaman, the other to bear the proud insignia of the Pioneer
Corps upon his lapels, his one pip, swagger cane, Sam Browne
and gloves – when had he ever had gloves? – much in evidence.
He had acquired more than gloves, however, drew himself up
at the sight of his old friend and, feeling a sudden physical
need as of old, enquired in the harshly articulated tones of the
South Wales Posh which we came to ridicule,

'I say, Bashie old man, where by is the pisshouse now?' Even
in the jokes there was evidence of change, and in the general
turmoil South Walians wandered and scattered, very often
settled elsewhere, the ablest generally leaving home. There was
little to keep them there if they were ambitious, and most left
without a qualm, especially if they were from the eastern
valleys. Perhaps they were lucky in that the ties that bound
them were less strong than those in the west where the Welsh

language was the central core of belonging, and there was no possibility of leaving. It was inevitable that Carwyn should come home. He was tied, bound hand and foot by the welcome chains of language and, of course, of rugby football, the milieu which was to give him his greatest happiness.
Not for him even the temporary agonies of the poet, T. H. Parry Williams:

> What do I care about Wales? It's just an odd chance
> That I live in her land. All she is on a map
> Is a sliver of earth in an off-beat corner
> Just a nuisance to those who believe in order.
> And who lives in this backwater, just tell me that?
> The refuse of humanity: for God's sake don't
> Cackle about entities, nations, countries . . .
> Plenty of those around, leave out Wales . . .*

This was a point made ironically and savagely. Carwyn would never even have asked the questions. It would never have occurred to him to leave out Wales. Had he been a scientist, or pursued some academic speciality whose practice required him to move, there might conceivably have been another story, but I doubt it. All his specialities would have come to fruition at home.

The summer of 1954 was a summer of letters, letters which he kept or, more likely, were kept for him since they arrived at his home in Cefneithin. Before he left the navy there was a letter from Arthur Fairfax, the Rugby League Scout who had travelled to see him at Taunton, probably after playing in a services match. It is self-explanatory:

> First of all, please allow me to express my appreciation of your frankness during our chat on Sunday. I trust that I also assisted you with all the information supplied

---

* transl. R. Gerallt-Jones, *'Hon'* ('This One') from *Poetry of Wales 1930-1970*, Gomer Press, 1974.

and gained from my 30 years experience as the principal agent of the League clubs. I have reported to the Oldham Club and will write to you again shortly.

Mr Fairfax also suggested that Carwyn contact Bryn Meredith, later the Wales and British Lions's hooker, who was about to be married and would be, said Mr Fairfax, 'a grand pal to accompany you to Oldham'. There is no suggestion that Carwyn ever considered the matter seriously, indeed the letter to be passed on to Bryn Meredith was never even sent, but it is possible that Carwyn was intrigued by the offer and would have liked to have known his price, although no other contact appears to have been made. Later, the President of Surrey Rugby Football Club, also the chairman of an insurance company, wrote to offer the managership of his Cardiff office at a salary three hundred pounds in excess of a young teacher's salary, but this was immediately rejected – Mrs James relegating him unseen to the status of a house-to-house agent 'with an insurance book'.

In the same summer, Carwyn's old headmaster, Llewellyn Williams, sent him a telegram when one of the Welsh teachers at Gwendraeth Grammar School left the staff. Naturally, his first thought was of his former head prefect and he wired before advertising the post – he wanted to be sure Carwyn was interested – though there is little doubt that the advertisement was framed to suit the special candidate. 'I shall be very glad to have you and shall do everything I can now to see that you are appointed.'

There was, however, an ominous note. 'There are others at work for other candidates.' To be on the safe side, the headmaster also included a list of governors of the school in his letter, the aldermen, councillors and notables of the district, and bade Carwyn canvass their support, adding that he would do the same himself.

No one familiar with Welsh life will doubt that this was normal procedure. It was a common practice for graduates and others to trail around the councillors' houses, offering themselves for inspection, the canvassing being regarded as an extra interview in deliberately informal circumstances. Those who did not canvass were in a less favourable, if not a hopeless position, and very often, those who refused to do so had relatives who acted on their behalf. Such activities, like the confessions of pregnant servant girls at inopportune moments, formed the staple diet of many Welsh short stories and plays, the line 'I will not canvass!' drawing warm applause from those who had suffered under the system. It was a local recruiting system for very local people, but at the same time there is little doubt that it drove many able young men away from Wales, particularly at a time when they had been distanced from such practices by military service and simply could not face it again. This revulsion against nepotistical party politicians became fairly widespread and led, in the opinion of many, to a process of unnatural selection – the natural selection of the unfittest! The South Wales of my youth was thus denuded of talent as much by these practices as by the attractions of other jobs elsewhere.

But few people were ignorant of the system, and it is clear that the headmaster, himself the son of a Brynamman Labour alderman, loyal to his pupil and clearly wanting him to succeed, thought it prudent to advise acceptance of traditional ways. When his former head prefect paid no heed, and was consequently unsuccessful, another candidate being preferred, there began, in my view, the hardening of an aspect of Carwyn's nature which led in turn to a rejection of officialdom and its attendant practices. The provincial party boss, thriving in a virtual one-party system on nepotism and the kind of patronage which expected much tugging of forelocks, was repulsive to him. This kind of man was later satirised by the nationalist singer Dafydd Iwan:

> I've been on the Education Committee since 1933,
> I know every Headmaster in the county, or rather,
> they know me!

Carwyn's reaction to this solitary setback was to have an effect which lasted for the rest of his life. I would often talk of my own, similar experiences, including one choice memory of entering an interview room to be greeted, 'Pontypridd has not helped you keep your Welsh, Mr Richards!' Yet again I was unsuccessful, though this particular interview had an intriguing difference: once the decision had been reached, the successful candidate was called in once more, but a junior clerk came hastily out of the interview room to the steps outside the council chamber and gave a thumbs-up sign across the road whereupon a hidden cyclist appeared from nowhere and hurtled away to bear the good news, probably to Mam sitting at home who could not wait to hear the news from the golden boy himself. In my own life, I came to be rejected often, and the phrase, 'the qualifications of another candidate were preferred', became a joke which I once repeated to a dying man, drawing a last smile to his lips. A South Walian, he understood the society he was leaving. I was a schoolmaster then, but a certain notoriety hung about me as a playwright and perhaps posed a slight threat to long-established fiefdoms.

The idea of the Welsh as promulgated in England fearless and radical, the champions of the poor and oppressed – is only half the story. In small places, unchallenged political power creates grubby nests where cosy improprieties fester. Such a society hates challenge, resents success, remains unchanged while its spokesmen mouth the desirable forward-sounding sentiments. It is the residual pool of no-talent, where all are afraid of the light, in which the challenger is immediately accosted with the single sentence, 'Who does he think he is?' – a question that is asked many times, usually in private and with deadly effect because the answer inevitably is, 'Not one of us!' It is the sentiment, never publicly voiced which, I am sure, lies behind many seemingly inexplicable decisions in public life.

Of course, I am writing about the experiences of my generation, not Carwyn's, and it would be foolish to pretend that famous rugby players and former head prefects are the only desirable candidates for any given post, or indeed to assume that there were not better men available – I do not know. The headmaster, however, had no doubts and on the night of Carwyn's rejection, he expressed himself forcibly on the matter to another distinguished ex-pupil, later to be Carwyn's obituarist in *The Times*, Professor John M. Thomas, FRS. What is clear, is that after this experience Carwyn never applied for any post as an ordinary schoolmaster where there was the slightest chance that he might be rejected. Implanted within him was a hostile notion of duly elected groups and this was intensified when he came across the Welsh Rugby Union which he saw as a similar group whose notables had a cast-iron resistance to the kind of changes he wanted. It was as if they, like the councillors and aldermen, had a built-in veneration and respect for the channels and processes which placed them in power, keeping them there, as he once put it in a speech at Llanelli's centenary dinner, 'until death do us part!' All such groups had a veneration for the social function, the traditions of formal junketing with a high incidence of endless soporific speeches, and one can quite easily imagine Carwyn substituting one group for the other. This was not entirely fair since the Welsh Rugby Union is clearly not a body allied to any political party, and in many ways it had no need to defend its considerable successes. But at the same time it was a group elected by the vote, given to lobbying and there was something about the voting procedure which Carwyn distrusted, especially when the same officials were repeatedly returned to power and began to hunt in packs. He saw them bearing down, not so much with sharpened teeth, but with glazed eyes made blank with incomprehension, as if the mere presence of numbers, in inverse ratio to intelligence, guaranteed a mindless herd. It was a prejudice, the sum of his feelings rather than his reason, and again and again in his life, except where he was known and loved, the vote was not his for the asking so that the prejudice remained and attracted understandable criticism and suggestions of arrogance which he promptly dispensed with by simply claiming, 'Well, I am arrogant!'

If Carwyn was irrational in some respects, the fact is he had an artist's impatience with the slow and tortuous processes whereby ordinary men seek laboriously to come to terms with their environment. His insights were inspirational. Merlin would not, could not canvass, nor bend the knee. Merlin was not ordinary and woe betide anyone in a sea of mediocrity who is not ordinary. He will suffer, and suffer Carwyn did although, being the kind of man he was, he retained many friends even at the heart of the rugby establishment which he never ceased to criticise. He even openly fostered the belief that he had been continually rejected by them which, on closer examination, is not as accurate as he would have had us believe.

In 1954, however, Merlin was only beginning his apprenticeship. The sorcery was to come. Shrugging off his failure at Gwendraeth, he soon found a temporary appointment at Queen Elizabeth Grammar School, Carmarthen, where he taught as a Welsh master for two years during the long-term absence of a permanent teacher. Among the pupils was Denzil Davies, later to be Labour MP for Llanelli and his political opponent. At Carmarthen, there is no doubt that the veneration of the school was guaranteed by the fact that the new Welsh master was playing rugby regularly for Llanelli and indeed, when he injured himself coaching the school second fifteen, we can imagine that dismay was universal when it was found out that he had made himself unavailable to play against Cardiff the following Saturday. You can almost hear the news being reported down the school corridors, 'Carwyn's out!' He is also remembered for the vigorous part he played in school eisteddfodau, but principally for the kudos he brought with him as a top-class rugby player. The Welsh fly-half position at this time was securely in the hands of Cliff Morgan and Carwyn was not securely in contention for international honours until 1958, four years later, by which time he was well established at Llandovery College.

The move to Llandovery College was an event in Carwyn's life that might be taken as the absolute reversal of the Gwendraeth processes. Although, as in Gwendraeth, he was wanted from the outset, his name was actually put forward by his mentors in Aberystwyth University when the Warden of Llandovery, Canon G. O. Williams (later Archbishop of Wales), asked for advice he wanted to recruit a Welsh master who would help him to revitalise the teaching of Welsh in the school. The implication is that he wanted the best man known to the university authorities and the name given to him was that of Carwyn Rees James. Llandovery College, an independent boarding school for boys, is described as 'an educational establishment of major importance in Wales for a hundred and thirty years', and Canon G. O. Williams specifically drew attention to the school's obligations to fulfil the Welsh language provisions contained in its original trust deed – its founder, Thomas Phillips, having stated that he was 'desirous of founding and endowing a Welsh School in the Diocese of St David's for the study and cultivation of the Welsh or Ancient British Language and Literature'.

The history of the college relates,

> In particular, the warden had made it clear – in contrast to so many of his predecessors – that one of Llandovery's main functions is to be a Welsh school, and although he was conscious of the difficulties involved in a country where only a minority were Welsh-speaking, he believed that there was a positive role for Llandovery 'in bridging the linguistic chasm'.*

Soon after Carwyn's arrival, the college became designated in *The Public Schools Year Book* as a school where: 'Welsh boys would study their own language, history and literature as part of a sound classical and liberal education.'

---

* W. Gareth Evans, *History of Llandovery College*, published by the Trustees, 1981.

In academic language this, to Carwyn, was the equivalent of the lance corporal's muttered aside as he passed through the main guard gate at Coulsdon four years before, 'You're playing Saturday!', and from the moment of his appointment in 1956 there began the busiest and most involved period of his life as a schoolmaster until 1968 when a similar invitation was extended to him by Trinity College, Carmarthen, when he was again specifically requested to apply for a post as a lecturer in Welsh studies.

There is no doubt that 'Chapel' Carwyn found Anglican ways much to his taste – his preference, perhaps, for a certain style. (We always quarrelled as to who had introduced the word 'insouciant' into his vocabulary. I claimed the honour, first using it to describe the classic Welsh fly-half, Glyn Davies, whom I also described as 'a High Churchman in his style of play'. My claim was rudely dismissed by Carwyn. Perhaps it was an archbishop.)

The Llandovery College history also records that many changes took place under the tenure of Canon Williams, one of which was that the teaching of Welsh was made compulsory, and although the school was criticised shortly after he left by HM Inspectorate who felt (in 1959) that the curriculum was better designed for the able minority than for the less able majority, there is no doubt that Carwyn was in his element and fully agreed with the warden whose concern was to ensure that the Welsh language played a prominent role in the life of the school. A future warden, R. Gerallt-Jones, expressed his own aims similarly: 'We are trying to foster Welshness – which I do not interpret in a purely linguistic sense – in such a way that a sympathetic understanding can emerge between Welsh and English pupils.'

These aims were probably unique to Llandovery College and would have been greeted with open-mouthed incredulity elsewhere in the principality, but if fostering Welshness – whatever that was – was interpreted in rugby football terms, it has to be said that Llandovery College was known for its

rugby team. Its sports master, T. P. Williams, was famous in
Wales as the mentor of such internationals as Vivian Jenkins
(later the rugby correspondent of *The Sunday Times*), Cliff Jones
(President of the Welsh Rugby Union in its centenary year),
and many others. T. P. Williams was a well-known schoolboy
coach who encouraged a fluent three-quarter game with fingertip passing (he once made his most famous protégé, Cliff Jones,
practise handling with a bar of soap), and Carwyn, who
became his assistant, always spoke of him with respect and
affection.

But good rugby schools were not uncommon in Wales and
in the matter of 'bridging the chasm' and 'fostering Welshness',
it is questionable whether the compulsory learning of Welsh
was the way to achieve it. This would certainly not have been
the case elsewhere and it is probably true to say that Welsh
medium schools, which had similar principles, only began to
succeed in later years when they were seen to have a certain
social cachet and, being on the whole much smaller than the
neighbourhood comprehensive schools, were preferred by
parents who were quick to see the opportunities presented to
bilingual children in the changed circumstances of the 1970s.
Casting a backward glance, it is still possible to see how in a
small enclosed community such as Llandovery, the declared
aims of the various wardens were filtered down into school
activities and harnessed to inter-house rivalries and competitions like eisteddfodau, all seriously engaging the attention of
pupils who did not leave at the end of the afternoon to return
to an environment indifferent to any consciously Welsh
aspirations. Nobody had to deliver newspapers after school
or indeed to assist the milkman before attending it.

Those who recall Carwyn's time at Llandovery inevitably
mention the success of the Welsh Society which he ran every
Tuesday throughout the winter, inviting visiting speakers to
address the boys in Welsh on chosen subjects. As the atmosphere was convivial and informal and its speakers usually
interesting, it became one of the most popular societies in the

college, and it is significant that even boys with a very poor command of the Welsh language were eager to attend.

From an educational point of view, the visiting firemen were all distinguished in their fields: a BBC producer to talk about broadcasting, a politician to talk of the history of Wales, a famous international to talk about rugby football, an entertainer on entertaining, a don on medieval poets and, undoubtedly the star attraction, the future Welsh coach Clive Rowlands addressing the assembled company on 'Rugby Motivation'. This all sounded excellent in the year's report of the college's activities, but a closer look reveals a well-known Jamesian practice for most of the visiting firemen were his friends; throughout his life, you were likely to be called upon at a moment's notice to present yourself to talk to this group or that. Carwyn was warm and appreciative of the gifts of his friends and this, together with his ability to play devil's advocate, created a friendly environment, very different from the classroom, in which to bring his pupils into contact with a wide range of people whom they might otherwise not have met.

All his life Carwyn had a capacity for getting the best out of people which I will try once again to define. From an early age, he made friends easily and quickly, partly because he guaranteed his undivided attention when it was needed, and partly because he increasingly began to need friends himself. One of his long-standing traits was the habit of devoting himself exclusively and wholeheartedly to a principal task in hand, be it friend or problem, to the absolute exclusion of all else. It was a central paradox of his nature, the conundrum of how a man who was so organised when it mattered, could be so disorganised when it didn't. The only analogy is the painter so obsessed that he does not notice how the bucket has become wrapped around his foot and clumps noisily about his studio, his total concentration on a major canvas leaving him blind to everything else. This aspect of his character became more noticeable later on in his life, but it is clear that at Llandovery he was sowing the seeds of a pattern of behaviour which was to remain with him.

At Llandovery College he is remembered with affection as a first-class teacher, inspirational and sometimes operatic when he gave forth of his literary enthusiasms, ignoring bells and timetables when in full flight, his voice rising and falling and more animated than it ever was to be in rugby dressing-rooms where he was always the calm man. He taught, when the mood took him, with passion. He was unquestionably a good disciplinarian but never worked at it, and as a housemaster he was able to give more time in crowded weeks than a man with the competing claims of a family. His results were excellent, the organisation of his work in the classroom meticulous as he set about revitalising the teaching of Welsh. The residential atmosphere suited him. It was a way of life. Importantly, domestic chores were taken care of, ash trays emptied on sight, and if his cars grew progressively untidier as he created what must have been his first back-seat office desk, he couldn't have managed without them as he was an inveterate traveller, taking parties of boys to cultural functions throughout Wales. The school soon began to send competing verse, drama and choral teams to young people's eisteddfodau at all levels and they were so successful that they made a name for themselves and the school, and probably attracted pupils who might not otherwise have entered the college. In short, Carwyn put Llandovery's Welsh hat in the ring and, on one occasion, he was so involved with the performance of these competing groups that he was physically sick, such was his identification and single-mindedness. In competition he was, as ever, ambitious, aggressive and successful, and since he was capped twice for Wales while at Llandovery, and regularly played for Llanelli in his first years there, the fullness of his life can easily be imagined. It was a time of his life when he was fully occupied, and those who knew him then can think of him only as a schoolmaster. It was his true forte.

His cigarette-smoking habits, by now pronounced, never

varied and the boys sometimes called him 'Kipper', noted his ritual breakfast, 'a coffee and a cough', and took care to put him in the right frame of mind with the obligatory copy of the *Western Mail* suitably folded to offer the sports page as his first sight of the day.

He was never perfect, but the imperfect man found time to cast his eyes on youthful schoolboy rugby talent elsewhere and he attempted unsuccessfully to recruit two young pupils to the school at an early age, Phil Bennett and Barry John. He believed in excellence, and when he saw it he knew it. If he leaned heavily on colleagues at times – 'Look here, you can do that because you're better than me at it!' – they seldom failed him. Neither did his house prefects fail when visiting lady friends showed a reluctance to leave, for the prefects knew when to interrupt with bogus calls to duty, unflattering but usually disguised by an eloquent excuse.

An over-riding memory of him shared by pupils and staff is as a man of constant informal conversations in the sitting-room rather than the classroom, always interested and always available to listen – 'somehow the rugby did not matter'. He suited Llandovery College and Llandovery College suited him, and probably at no other time in his life did he find such ful-filment outside of rugby football, and then only in the intensity of fierce competition, success and victory, and the inevitable euphoria which followed.

Carwyn the Blameless, Carwyn the Head Prefect, Carwyn sidestepping on shadows in a sunlit park as a very young player, 'so little body, so much mind, and big ears that stuck out!' – the wraith matured, not into the great international playing legend but as Kipper, the inspirational conversation-alist, the listener by day and by night, for he was by now also known as The Owl since his late nights never varied.

The respective wardens made their educational aims known in language both precise and imprecise. In 'fostering Welshness' they might have spawned a new limpid strain of influenza. Instead, they got a very human being, drifting along among clouds of cigarette smoke, a convivial character who invited all his friends to the party wherever the party happened to be. In teaching, he took the poet out of the set book and introduced him as a friend; in competition he wanted the best, everything you had to give; and to the college, whose playing fields and the Welsh society he made ever more popular, he inveigled his friends – he wanted to share them and their skills. It became another lifelong habit.

In Llandovery there was not a councillor in sight, real or imaginary and, until the last year or so, no votes were required or sought. Why, then, did he leave? 'If I had stayed another year,' he once told me, 'I would have been there for the rest of my life.' He wanted a change, sought one, succeeded, and then regretted it, but he was to return at intervals. Once he confused everyone by returning to Aberystwyth University one summer in an immaculate and bright red Jaguar car, 'a jewel in the town', and promptly beginning an MA thesis on the works of the sixteenth-century poet, Edward ap Raff. Like a Welsh Raffles, he always liked to return, in this instance only as an amateur cracksman for he never completed the job. There were others waiting.

*   *   *

After Llandovery College Carwyn moved, once more by invitation, to Trinity College, Carmarthen, where he became a lecturer in Welsh Studies to teachers in training. The vice principal, Miss Irene James, had taught him in Gwendraeth Grammar School; the Head of the Department of Welsh and Drama, Miss Norah Isaac, wanted him for her own department; and Carwyn had frequently brought parties of Llandovery boys to see productions of Welsh plays put on by the drama department some of whose students went on, not to teach, but to fill drama posts in the lucrative fields opened up exclusively to bilingual candidates when Welsh language broadcasting increased its output in the 1970s. Carwyn had on several previous occasions been asked to apply, but refused on the grounds that he wanted to stay on at Llandovery until he had seen his original students through a complete six-year course in Welsh, an estimable reason and one that would have made him all the more desirable. Even by refusing, he was adding to his reputation. When his application eventually arrived in 1968, probably one of the untidiest in the history of the college, the spidery handwriting in Welsh with a pencilled translation immediately added in English by the registrar's office, the names of his referees were the two poets, Gwenallt and T. H. Parry Williams. It was the Welsh equivalent of W. H. Auden and T. S. Eliot recommending a protégé for some minor English teacher training college.

These two Welsh writers also formed the subject matter of Carwyn's most successful lectures which he repeated endlessly and he soon became a favoured lecturer. He was also fortunate in having a benevolent head of department who allowed him to deal with those aspects of Welsh literature he most cared about. As so often happened in his life, he was at his best when left to develop his enthusiasms, preferably not too early in the morning, emerging enthusiastically in the more sociable hours when conversation was more likely to be spontaneous. He was not expected to take an official interest in the college rugby team, although he helped out when required. It was probably an easier life than that of a public schoolmaster and house-master, and during his six years there he managed to develop all his interests. Threads came together and other worlds began to beckon.

Even before he arrived, he had been asked to stand as Plaid Cymru candidate for the expected parliamentary election at Llanelli where the veteran Labour MP James Griffiths was retiring. His name had also been submitted to the Four Home Unions Committee as one of the two Welsh Rugby Union recommendations for the coach for the 1971 British Lions tour of New Zealand and Australia. He was already known as a broadcaster, making increasingly frequent broadcasts in Welsh and in English for BBC Wales where he was one of the pioneers of Welsh sports broadcasting, helping to define a Welsh vocabulary of sport. He had also agreed to coach Llanelli Rugby Football Club at the invitation of Peter Rees, the chairman, after a discussion with his committee and senior players, among them Clive and Alan John, brothers of Barry John and, as if this was not enough, he was soon a deacon and secretary of Tabernacle Chapel, Cefneithin, where he was now living once more in the new bungalow which the children had built for their aged parents.

The threads, each one of which might have been a major occupation, are perhaps an indication of Carwyn's standing as much as his abilities. Later in life there were those who felt that he fell victim to the dilemma of the freelance journalist who dares not refuse a single assignment and consequently ruinously overworks, but he always had to deal with extortionate demands upon his time. He was that rare individual whose presence enhances both a moment and a movement and there was hardly an organisation in Welsh-speaking Wales which did not claim his allegiance. He was in so many ways all that Welsh Wales asked for, unswerving in his loyalties to chapel, hearth and home, and ever approachable. It is a small world, a world where everyone seems to know everyone else, and Carwyn's life resembled the voyage of a ship, at first making small forays around a known coastline with many harbours, then venturing further, all the while gathering momentum and taking on board an unshakeable cargo which could not be jettisoned. Once you met him and a mutual regard was established, you signed on for the voyage. His friends, particularly from those early years, always regarded him as a precious spirit permanently on tap, just as he did them. Because he was so involved with the communities which claimed him and moved deftly from one group to another as the demands increased, legends grew up, no doubt based on fact. There were now Carwyn stories, Carwyn the Chapel Secretary who always preferred the telephone to the letter, committing the classic mistake of double-booking ministers for the Sunday service and palliating his mistake with the ready supply of scarce rugby international tickets for those he made into enforced spiritual reserves by his negligence; Carwyn the Deacon who seldom sat in the 'Big Seat' reserved for deacons, and when challenged by a Reverend friend as to what he was doing in the back seat of the chapel, replied, 'Planning tactics for next Saturday!' Saturday loomed as large in his thinking as Sunday, obvious days of well-defined activity, and it is clear that even before his appointment as British Lions coach in 1969, he was a man in demand, particularly in Welsh Wales where he might have been a propagandist's stereotype of a local hero, computer-produced for the admiration of his clan. He also often confused the stereotype for, notoriously helpless in the kitchen, he is said to have cooked a superb meal for his pupils at a Welsh youth rally at the Urdd Camp at Llangrannog, a circumstance unimaginable to his friends in later life just as unbelievable as the vision of him scurrying around the Naval hut at Coulsdon tidying up in order to win points for his team. But that was Carwyn, always capable when he wanted to be.

There are also ironies. He was probably the only public schoolmaster to broadcast on Plaid Cymru's illegal radio transmitter and subsequently received a solemn warning from one member of the broadcasting establishment. Within the space of a few months, he had luncheon in the exclusive East India Club in London, and then in North Wales took part in a demonstration on the road outside the stone plinth commemorating the death of Llewellyn the Last, 'the last true Prince of Wales', at Cilmeri. This was a counter-investiture demonstration held under the watchful eyes of the Special Branch shortly before the official investiture of Prince Charles at Caernarvon. At the East India Club he charmed the representatives of the Four Home Rugby Unions meeting into selecting him as manager and coach for the British Lions tour, while at Cilmeri he was keeping the same company as he had years before at Trawsfynydd when he protested at the continued existence of a military presence on a gunnery range.

Six days after the Cilmeri demonstration, two young Welshmen blew themselves up, presumably by accident while laying an explosive charge at government offices at Abergele, and an English schoolboy was maimed – but these were acts of violence which neither Carwyn nor his party would ever have condoned. At the same time, he was always prepared to put himself on the line with his fellow Plaid members and the Welsh Language Society who, in particular, regarded the investiture as little more than a media circus. Had he been a lecturer at Aberystwyth University during that period of Prince Charles's short residence, it is very likely his telephone would have been tapped, and while it is probable that nothing more sinister than details of his consistent demand for international tickets from his club would have emerged, his nationalist activities, albeit mild and supportive, were unacceptable to most Welshmen who welcomed the investiture and later conclusively rejected all demands for a devolved parliament.

'Carwyn James speaks for Wales', proclaimed his Plaid Cymru election brochure. It was true, and it was not true. In political terms he spoke for *his* Wales only. It was a dream that was never universally shared by the broad mass of the people who were simply not interested in his memories or his aspirations. But the Carwyn James who *played for* Wales was another person in the public mind, as was the coach who first addressed himself to the problems of playing against New Zealand with a West Wales team in 1967. If he saddened nationalist hearts by coaching a Llanelli side against the visiting Springboks in 1969, he made up for it in part by refusing to watch the game, remaining in the dressing-room throughout the match and also declining to attend the function later. It was a unique, if somewhat bizarre and ineffective protest, intended to express his detestation of apartheid, a generally approved view in Welsh political circles. The picture of him alone in the dressing-room, chain smoking as he listened to the radio, his vigil only once disturbed by the footsteps of Ray Williams, then the Welsh Coaching Organiser who was bidden to come *immediately on half-time* to give the most informed opinion available, is slightly comic. Compared to stands made by other nationalists on Welsh issues, it was a very minor demonstration, although no one who knew Carwyn then could doubt the intensity of his views. (He later modified his opinions and visited South Africa as a journalist several times, to the dismay of his politically-minded friends.)

From these years on, there is little doubt that rugby football was to engage Carwyn's attention more and more. It was in 1969 that he first stood for election as a district representative to the Welsh Rugby Union and in the same year he was considered with Clive Rowlands as assistant manager and coach for the Welsh tour to Australia and New Zealand. As in the parliamentary election he was unsuccessful, although after failing at the plebian hustings at home, there was success to come when he was nominated for the British Lions tour of New Zealand and Australia in 1971. There is no doubt that in his mind this was the plum job. There is no doubt either that the two Welsh representatives on the Four Home Unions Committee, Ken Harris and Hermas Evans, had a high regard for him. Carwyn the Contender now emerged spruce from the Hilton Hotel, having fortified himself with a Russian language performance of a Chekhov play at the Aldwych on the previous evening, and summoned a taxi to the East India Club at St James. Who can say whether or not he addressed himself as he had so confidently addressed his many teams in the past. 'We are going to win this one!' or, better still, 'We're going to hit this lot very hard from the start!'

There were eight candidates for the two jobs as manager and coach and during the conversation at lunch there was one cryptic sentence which was to be recalled later.

'Of course, you know, I don't believe in all this bloody nonsense about coaching!'

There were, it seemed, councillors everywhere!

When asked inevitably about his political candidature with

the election a fortnight away, Carwyn had an answer ready. He probably rightly felt that his Plaid convictions were less offensive in London than they would have been in Cardiff. Of the interview, he later wrote:

> I made two points: that I was competing with all my might to win the seat, even though the Labour majority was well over 20,000; that in the current issue of the *Llanelli Star*, the odds quoted against the Plaid Cymru candidate were ten thousand to one against, so I politely offered to take the committee's pounds back home in the hope that they would all make a quick ten thousand! No offers were forthcoming but I got the job. Needless to say, I didn't win the seat, but I did manage 'a saved my deposit job' with eight and a half thousand votes, the average gate at Llanelli's Stradey Park.

Although unsuccessful in the election, the very fact of his standing must have had some influence on the Llanelli Labour party since they appointed a former pupil of Carwyn's, a young Welsh-speaking lawyer, Denzil Davies, in preference to older men. Nationalism was at the time thought to be on the upgrade: Gwynfor Evans had won Carmarthen from Labour, Winnie Ewing had won Hamilton in Scotland, and there were swings away from Labour in safe seats in the East Wales bi-elections. Everywhere the young Labour candidate went to canvass in the rugby villages of Pontyberem, Tumble, Hendy and in Llanelli itself, his opponent, Carwyn James, was well known. But Denzil Davies need not have worried. He obtained his highest ever majority, probably because the Tory vote was low, and was in as little danger as the rugby union representatives in the district elections in 1969. Carwyn never got the votes that mattered, not even in the parish council elections in Cefneithin.

Merlin ran well for the line, but not for office in any capacity. Running for office meant canvassing and he was not even a walker in this respect, so it was the assembled gentlemen at the East India Club in St James whose collective nod brought him the most exciting time of his life.

Now New Zealand beckoned. He welcomed it and later wrote, 'There was a certain nakedness in the New Zealand countryside, you felt you could taste the earth – almost as if you were back in Wales.'

Nothing precious about James the Tactics!

Chapter Six

James the Tactics

Had Carwyn written the story of his own life, there is no doubt what its title would have been, and indeed, he pencilled it several times on the manuscripts which he never completed – *A Rugger Man*. It was taken from an obscure Welsh short story by W. Aldred Thomas which he knew by heart and sometimes recited aloud.

> I'm a rugger man. You'd just as well have it straight! There may be other games – I suppose there are one or two somewhere, but there's only one man's game – rugger.

While this drew roars of approval in smoke-filled club rooms, the fact is it represented only the tip of Carwyn's enthusiasm. There is little doubt that he was the most unusual of men and brought to rugby football concepts and passions, and a persona which was uniquely Welsh, all of which reflected his whole attitude to life. In particular, he had his own standards of excellence and a coherent picture of what might be, the artist's glimpse of total possibilities – this an inspirational vision as if, like Shelley, he was aware of the fading coals of creation, of the first moment of seeing which ever after is never quite so bright and the task executed is somehow always paler than the brilliance of the first concept. If it sounds far-fetched to apply such a comparison to a mere game, the answer is, of course, that Carwyn never saw rugby football as a mere game. He would reflect, for example, on the careers of such players as the Lions's wing threequarter Gerald Davies, whose lovely running and daring brought him every honour in the game, and then say, 'His potential has seldom been realised.' It was not that he was unaware of exactly how brilliant Gerald had been, but there was, in Carwyn's mind, more that could have been achieved, aesthetic patterns of play which he had glimpsed and in which the great players might be fully utilised.

It was this vision of what might be which made him the coach of coaches, as if like an artist, he saw the drama ahead already staged but was waiting for the plot and principal characters to fill it out, all to combine to form an almost theatrical ensemble in which victory played only a part. Victory was important, but not by itself enough, and it was this conception of possibilities which was so fully realised in the kind of rugby football played by his returned Lions in the match of the decade at the Cardiff Arms Park when the Barbarians played New Zealand at the conclusion of the All Black visit in 1973. In many people's minds this was a kind of fifth test match between the 1971 Lions and their old adversaries, even though principal players like Barry John, Gerald and Mervyn Davies were missing. In that game, probably the most widely televised ever, the achievements of previous years were manifested both in the skills shown and the enthusiasms generated, particularly amongst the young. It represented the ultimate in excitement and skill, the excellence which Carwyn revered in the qualities of both teams, two being required to make the bargain. In New Zealand earlier, the battle had, of course, been closer, the touring Lions having seldom been allowed to play with such continuous flair, but the ultimate result, the test victories and unbeaten provincial record represented for Carwyn a high point which – his club successes apart meant that in rugby football terms his life ever after was an anticlimax.

In New Zealand, he and his team had broken the stranglehold of the southern hemisphere in rugby terms and were the first ever British Lions side to win a test series. They made history, but in Carwyn's life it was as if, having been the inspiration of that pinnacle, the heights scaled were so great that from the crowning moment there could only be a descent. There is no doubt that this was a peak which affected his whole life, changed his mode of living, perhaps because he had lived it so intensely, he, the dreamer who had realised his dreams, particularly as he was never again in a position to achieve them on so grand a scale. But whatever may be said by way of regret at so short a life, he had no regrets himself and regarded his part in the success of others throughout his life as his chief source of satisfaction.

Towards those who selected him, to his tour manager, Doug Smith, his captain, John Dawes, and to the whole company of players, he retained a feeling of gratitude which lasted until his death, and if there is one remark made by him on the whole tour which completely expresses his own pleasure, it was the simple question with which he complimented the Irish centre, Mike Gibson, after a superb performance against Wellington, 'When have you ever played better than that?' It was a question that did not require an answer. Like the Dodo in *Alice in Wonderland*, he wanted everyone to have prizes. In rugby football, he took as much care as he could to see that they got them, and perhaps the most profound tribute to him is also the simplest, his captain's: 'He was a man who gave so much of himself to other people. He never asked for anything for himself. In rugby terms, he was on a different plane to other people. He was ever learning.'

Maybe only those who shared in his victory really know how much he gave them: the outsider can only guess at the particulars, the confidence inspired in others, the ready ear of the ever-willing listener. In the Lions tour he created the role of senior professional in the team, a role first filled by the Irish prop-forward Ray McCloughlin whom Carwyn never ceased to be grateful towards and to praise, an example also of his own eagerness to be pupil when he felt it necessary. There was a good deal he already knew about his team, particularly the Welsh players, and for months before the tour he was busy compiling a dossier on the New Zealand players and clubs which was evidently so complete that he was able to pick provisional British sides for specific matches weeks ahead, before the party had even played a single game in New Zealand. As if this was not enough, he also paid a short visit to Manchester United to ask Dave Sexton about his methods of conducting training schedules, and travelled to Wigan Rugby League Club to study their techniques. Next he invited Ray Williams, the Welsh coaching organiser who had recently returned from New Zealand, to address the assembled party at Eastbourne before their departure, once again gathering in all the friends he could to help with the task in hand. In John Dawes's words, 'In rugby terms, Carwyn never left anything to chance. When we left Eastbourne, we were a united party.'

In recall, players on the tour can still trace the threads of his influence, some of them expressing their surprise at the gentleness of his nature. He was a man who seldom raised his voice, and whilst some had fears that being so obviously Welsh he might be expected to be partisan, it was not so, nor ever felt to be so. He expressed his philosophy on this score himself:

> I remember well, the day I met my '71 Lions for the first time. The very first thing I said to them was, 'Look here, be your own man. Express yourself, not as you would at the office, but as you would at home. I don't want Irish-men to pretend to be English, or Englishmen to be Celts, or Scotsmen to be anything less than Scots. You each have an ultimate quality to give to the team and you must know that you are able to express yourself in your own special unique way, both on the field and off it.'

Nothing could be clearer and in his mind he saw the team as a glorious fusion of national differences, perhaps because he was so completely confident of his own identity. It left him undisturbed to concentrate on the task in hand. He had clear views on the coach's role which can seldom have been better expressed:

On tour, as coach, you must happily concentrate every minute of the day. You must be a full person and aware that you are surrounded by different kinds of people. If one person likes soccer, you must know all about his favourite team, or cricket, when the scores are sent over from home. If music, you must have his same ear. Simply, you must know what drink he likes to drink.

It is a simple declaration of aims, but nevertheless a formidable task, and yet, as anyone who knew Carwyn can testify, it was a part of his nature to get to the essence of people and it did not apply only to his players, but to the children of his friends, and those with whom he worked no matter what position they held. He made it his business to know people's preferences and tastes, and he had a genuine interest in his colleagues as if every face that confronted him represented a puzzle to which he sought to find the answer. It applied to cameramen, technicians, secretaries, liaison officers, colleagues, no less than players, and the very mildness of his nature assisted him since the same intense interest emanating from a more forceful character would have been offensive. In this sense, he was man-made to be a confidant, a counsellor, and few people who knew him well had the slightest reservation about confiding in him, whether he was in or out of his tracksuit. Those who had doubts about their fitness or some aspect of their play would not hesitate to tell him, perhaps prompting him to be the creator of the sporting clinic, an extra session for concentration on specific skills, the therapy as important as the therapist who loved a poetic quotation and believed with Goethe that while correction achieves much, encouragement achieves more.

With Barry John, who almost doubled the scoring record for a visiting Tourist in New Zealand, Carwyn had a special relationship which, in rugby terms, was all the more special, not because Barry had once collected balls on the village field for his hero when playing, but, as Barry says, in that he had watched Carwyn as a player for Llanelli, when he learned to study his positional play off the ball. If Barry played rugby in a natural and instinctive way, his game uniquely his own, it was a game which began with his nose pressed against the railings, with him asking questions as to why his own favourite Llanelli player stood where he did, kicked when he did, or positioned himself in anticipation of moves that no one else had thought of. This is another way of saying that the rugger man had done it all himself at one time or another, a qualification that he modestly forgot to mention in his definition of the coach's qualifications. Importantly, in Barry John's words,

> He made me think, just as he made all of us think and if there was one time he raised his voice on the paddocks all over New Zealand, it was the number of times when he told people – forwards in particular – 'Think! If you're beaten – fair enough – but if you're beaten when you haven't thought about something – you can't be helped.'

For Gerald Davies, Carwyn's skill was not just that he knew the game inside and out, but he knew people, and there are no coaching certificates which guarantee that.

> There were no national differences. Everybody liked him. Because he was so true to himself, he was simply himself – always – and people respected him for that. Although he was very much a Welshman, nobody thought about it. He never pushed his identity and his silences were very much a part of him. There are other coaches who would have been much too brash and over-confident – you couldn't have lived with them for three months on tour. He also kept himself apart when he wanted to, and yet he deliberately made it his business to mix with everyone in an informal and casual way. Every one of the thirty players felt they had an intimate relationship with him. To the English and Irish players,

he cut across the accepted understanding of what a coach ought to be – loud and forthright – he was not at all like that. He just made you think.

The same final sentence occurs again and again in such re-collections. Carwyn practised what he preached, treating every player as an individual, ever mindful of the pressures, even of the need to get away from conventional training, and this is demonstrated in his training schedules which always offered variety. He once said,

> Coaching means organisation and the more highly organised you are as a team, the more flexible you can be. Without organisation, you are not able to call the shots. Quite simply, if one accepts the premise that rugby is a complex game, then the duty of the coach is to resolve the complexities into simplicities.

This is the teacher speaking, but then there were the qualities of the man summed up by Barry John:

> Without him, it's very questionable if we would have done so well. He got from everybody, a tremendous respect – doctors, dentists, fitters, turners, miners – total respect, and that's an incredible achievement so that in the end, he gave players such belief, they were prepared to go out there and get hurt for him. There was never a game when he hadn't given his all. And he never patronised – never.

Those who knew Carwyn in New Zealand remember him at his peak, brisk, cheerful, immaculate and totally immersed in his task, and from the moment of his team's triumphant return to be greeted as no other team had been, his rugby life was lived socially with the same intensity. In the next four years he promptly went on to demonstrate the same skills with Llanelli

whose successes in Welsh cup competitions became mono-
tonous as they were repeated year after year. The famous victory
of his club over the touring All Blacks was crowned at the end
of the tour by the famous Barbarians game when Carwyn
addressed the players, reminding them once more of what they
had achieved and what could still be achieved. It was a period
in his life when success seemed to come automatically to those
associated with him, a high point of activity and acclaim which
extended like a plateau upon which he stood puffing away
at the inevitable cigarette, conspicuous only by his unobtrusiveness. He rode it unflappable, but only by acceding to
everybody's requests.

Looking back now, it is not difficult to see how the demands
upon his time began to increase, nor to isolate the strains upon
him, for at first little happened which had not happened
before, except that the multiplicity of demands slowly began
to make him both victim and conqueror. He had become, in
the rugby-playing countries of the world, in Gwynfor Evans's
words, 'the best known Welshman in the world' and this was
immediately apparent in the havoc caused in the day-to-day
schedules of the telephone operators at Trinity College,
Carmarthen, where he returned to take up his lecturing duties.
There were days when half the world seemed to be clamouring
for an interview on the other end of a telephone line. Walking
through a school playground to supervise some student on
teaching practice, his appearance would always cause a stir
in a rugby-playing population. The man fêted and brought
home to Cefneithin a hero could never be anonymous again,
no matter how little he had changed himself. In Wales, as in
England, he had become a focus for acclaim and now so many
things happened which were natural and proper attempts to
honour a hero when taken singly, but, when added up,
amounted to a series of pressures which his good nature
inevitably encouraged. It was appropriate that he should
be elected to prestigious bodies, for no man seemed better

qualified to preserve the Welsh language, to sit upon the University Council of Wales or the Sports Council, or to grace this body or that. But this was not all. In a real sense, it was the story of his life for he was once more 'playing on Saturday', except that now his desirability meant weeks of Saturdays with a score of different venues. If there was one thing lacking in his life, it was another unobtrusive immaculate figure in the dressing-room, his own coach, the cool mentor who could think ahead and pick the games to be played by the star. But there was no such person and Carwyn went obligingly from day to day doing everybody's bidding.

But there were not just the formal occasions, usually all away games, there was also fun and, taking the sting out of the volume of invitations to speak at rugby clubs in England and Wales, he teamed up for a short while with a then relatively unknown Max Boyce to provide an evening of rugby theory and rugby fun for those lucky clubs whose secretaries were persistent. Where else but Wales, one might ask, could a more complete rugby evening have been provided by such a double act? Max Boyce remembers Carwyn as supportive, a warm friend who valued the social content of his more serious songs, who urged him, as always, to be himself, shrugging off the pious criticisms of the occasional puritanical nationalist who could not take a Welsh joke. As with so many of Carwyn's friends, in recall, acts of kindness to unknown people spring first to mind, prompting his memorial ballad, 'What can you say about Carwyn?'

You could not add up the sum of the man without remembering numberless such acts, his ever-available car, his immediate readiness to provide a spare pair of trousers for a technician who unexpectedly found himself under a plate of curry. It was not so much that Carwyn had no side, but that he was the first at your side even in such an insignificant moment of embarrassment – all this a conundrum to those who found him aloof.

He could also make larger gestures as when he, together

with Barry John, recruited their rugby friends to provide a bonanza match, a nucleus of the returned Lions versus a Welsh side, Carwyn James's XV v Barry John's XV at the Cardiff Arms Park. The occasion was a celebration of the jubilee of the Welsh youth movement, the *Urdd*, whose members declare, 'I shall be faithful to Wales, to fellow man, and to Christ'. This is a simple motto which encapsulates a Jamesian philosophy, the simple man accepting simple declarations. The *Urdd* found themselves richer by fourteen thousand pounds, a sizeable sum unlikely to be raised by any other source, although the match marked the last appearance of Barry John at fly-half and the beginning of a period of national mourning for the end of his career, except of course by Phil Bennett who was already grooming himself in the inevitable Llanelli stable.

But these were good works, an offshoot of fame. At around this time, to compound the delight of his nationalist friends, no sooner had he arrived home and re-established himself than he refused the proffered MBE, the governmental salute for his contribution to the rugby tour. Then, very shortly afterwards, he found himself President of the Day at the Royal National Eisteddfod at Haverfordwest where he launched a subtle attack on the other Wales, the Wales indifferent to its language and culture, for the most part the grass roots of the rugby Wales. It had, he implied, lost its racial memory, aided and abetted by the cold impersonal hand of an administration which did not belong. This was the essential Carwyn, stepping down from one kind of fame to create another, now waspish and accusing, with a rapier thrust at those MPs, who changed their political colours 'like animals every winter', a jab too at educationists who neglected the Welsh past – 'Let the directors of education blush!' For nationalists – he spoke to a converted audience – it was a reaffirmation of faith but this was not a case of Carwyn returning to the fold. He had never left it and was now adding spice to his reputation, substituting the scholar's gown for the well-worn tracksuit.

On the platform he made a pious plea for a permanent eisteddfod home, or rather for four permanent buildings which would replace the travelling pavilion and remain behind to be centres of the arts where all Welshmen would be welcome, once the great Welsh jamboree was over and the English tongue was predominant again. He was serious, he was concerned, and more than anything his heart was with the young activists who were unafraid of demonstration, who were by their actions conducting a renaissance of the spirit which owed nothing to these councillors 'who refused to accept anything in Welsh or relating to Welsh'. He could not resist that last thrust, even if the councillors were doing no more than expressing the sentiments of those who elected them.

Carwyn was listened to with rapt attention as Wales's best-known Welshman restating his own values and encouraging the young demonstrators in their attack on an establishment which they saw as uncaring, and it was one more public indication of where his deeply felt interests lay. He was also once more standing in line with those like Gwenallt whom he had always revered. If there was anarchy in the world, there was order on the eisteddfod platform where he felt himself free to point the way ahead and to pay tribute to the Welsh past. 'A nation's memory is its history and a nation keeps its memory alive by making sure that its history is a part of its education.' There was an added piquancy in his quotation from the winning Crown poem which was written by his friend Dafydd Rowlands:

> Early we sat to chant the shape of history
> We learned about Lizzie Next Door and knew nothing
>   about Mam.
> Ten Sixty-six, Ten Sixty-six . . .
> And in the rhythmic beat there was no place for
>   Llanfair-ym-Muallt,
> A crooked rhyme about yesterday. The Spanish Armada –
> Fifteen Eighty-eight . . .

And the galleon from Llanrhaeadr-ym-Mochnant sailed
   heavy
With the wealth of verses, and we knew only
About some fellow playing bowls . . .*

'The man', according to the Italian newspaper headline, 'who
said no to the Queen of England' was intending no dis-
courtesy to the Queen, nor indeed was he casting aspersions
on Admiral Drake, long dead in his hammock below, but you
would need a potted history to be aware, as the faithful were,
that Llanrhaeadr-ym-Mochnant was the incumbency of Bishop
William Morgan, the translator of the Bible into Welsh in 1588,
an act of immense historical importance in Wales, because
without the translation it is likely that the Welsh language
would have disintegrated into a series of mutually unintel-
ligible dialects. Simply, it gave the Book and with it a literary
culture to a people whose ruling class had deserted them for
the attractions of Tudor England, anglicising themselves with
indecent speed. In the absence of the aristocracy who were
followed hotfoot by the educated, professional and administrative classes (the first and most U of the London Welsh), a
decaying squirearchy and an impoverished peasantry were
left far behind. Now, in Bishop Morgan's translation, they
found a means for the survival of their language in a society
where fundamental differences of class were almost non-
existent. Essentially democratic, it was to find its echoes much
later in the tumultuous urban society of proletarian South
Wales, and both contributed to make Wales far less class-
conscious than England. There was always a time when the
Welsh were non-deferential and to cock a snook at 'Lizzie next
door', no less than at some 'fellow playing bowls', was as
natural to Carwyn as to his audience. Indeed, he was never
happier than when preaching to the converted, and his speech,
passionate and witty – 'They tell me the best method of
defence is to attack!' – was tumultuously received.

---

* Dafydd Rowlands, *Dadeni* (Renaissance).

It was the kind of performance which led many nationalists to imagine the place he might have carved for himself as an activist, and later to regret the duality of his nature which made him the kind of man who could step down from such a platform, the applause ringing in his ears, to enquire urgently if anyone had heard of Llanelli's performance in an away game. (It was, as it happens, an enquiry which he made on one of the last telephone calls of his life.) He was usually one step ahead of himself, of his current interest, his immediate success, his mind probing forwards, although at the back of it rugby football was never far away from his thoughts, complain as he sometimes did with an addict's mock regret. There are those who think he was the victim of his own talents, but they forget how brilliantly he succeeded at the things he cared about most. Carwyn as President of the Day at the Royal National Eisteddfod was no less successful or welcome than he was when appearing as a journalist or broadcaster. When he was admitted in flowing white robes to the select company of bards at the Gorsedd, it was as it should be.

But those who saw him as a politician were, in my view, mistaken. He was not a political animal and his nationalism was an expression of his depth of feeling about his own immediate past which extended back through literature and folk memory into a world which I only dimly perceived. What to me was at best picturesque and antiquarian, inevitably pastoral, a part of a childhood dream, at worst puritanical, narrow and inhibiting, was to him the good society and he had a concept of a social inheritance from an older way of life which was denied to most of his generation who were moulded, like myself, by different forces. The short story writer, D. J. Williams, expressed a view that was close to Carwyn's heart:

> Territorially, my family's inheritance has got smaller over the centuries, until it has almost vanished entirely in my own time. But this has never worried me in the

least, since I feel that I have somehow been allowed to keep something that is dearer in my sight than land or possessions – namely the consciousness of the ancient values of our fathers, together with a feeling of responsibility for their continuance. There is, in this feeling, a touch of Welsh citizenship that has not been killed by long oppression and violence, something that wholly unfits me to be a loyal citizen to any other authority. All loyalty is false that is not based on consent and on moral justice.

Carwyn believed in the upright man and he never wavered in his conclusion that without some form of self-government the Welsh people would never be able to protect and develop their moral and material resources. (He also told the playwright Colin Welland that if Wales had her own government, it would have been socialist for fifty years!) When the Welsh people rejected the opportunity for even a devolved form of government, to him it was like the beginning of the long night. That they did so because they were long estranged from and indifferent to the cultural values he held dear, and were probably against an increase in government of any political complexion, did not really occur to him, perhaps because he did not identify with those who did not speak Welsh, except on personal terms.

This was the paradox. The miner's son had grown away from his roots, his social status was not easily identifiable in a conventional sense, and it is this essential difference that was the most complex strand of his being. One of the ironies of Carwyn's life was that the game which meant so much to him, its history and the way it was played and organised, owed little to the pastoral Welsh life which he so admired, and yet it was the one unifying force in the fragmented society of modern Wales which offered him a platform for his talents. Politics did not, except in a notional sense, and neither did rugby politics, but that is a separate issue.

What made Carwyn so unique was that although he crossed most of the boundaries which confronted him, the little boy looking over the wall at Cefneithin at the rugby field from the shelter of his father's arms, had little choice, given his talents, but to become a rugby man because it was such a Welsh aspiration and as powerful in its attractions as any other aspect of Welsh life. In rugby football, there was no need to apologise nor to make excuses, nor was Wales 'a sliver of land in an off beat corner', but held a deserved place amongst the nations. There was also total national commitment and a widespread social approval, and whatever erosions ate away at the national inheritance, rugby football maintained its place as the national game.

No one saw this more clearly than Colin Welland, a friend of Carwyn's in later life, who saw what he describes as a South Lancashire parallel and was always aware that Carwyn's quixotic gentleness was unexpected in a rugby environment. 'He was like somebody beamed down from the starship Enterprise as a child to grow up in rugby-mad Wales – like a flower in a vegetable garden full of carrots and leeks. He couldn't just be a homely vegetable.' The mystery was that with all his gentleness, he survived to succeed brilliantly and, what is more, to create on the broadest of Welsh canvasses.

There was another factor, in that rugby football was a game in which all the people could participate because, from its inception, its South Walian pioneers had deliberately taken an essentially egalitarian stand. If the galleon of Llanrhaeadr-ym-Mochnant was but a boat from an unpronounceable place to most of Carwyn's contemporaries, those same contemporaries and their antecedents had formed the rugby clubs and the kind of society which grew up around the coal valleys and ports. It was that egalitarian society which needed and created rugby football, eventually accepting it as a national game and imbuing it with a national and local importance it was never intended to have. It also, at times, became a reflection of that society, taking on, even before the installations of floodlights, an intensely theatrical aspect as its heroes and villains cavorted in accordance with the wishes of their proletarian audience whose participation, no less than that of the players, was one proof at least that they were not as ordinary as the machines seemed intent on making them.

And in the society which created all this, you would have been hard put to find even the vestiges of that peculiar Victorian morality which prevailed elsewhere, for example, when Grace Kelly's father, albeit a millionaire, was prevented from rowing at Henley on the grounds that he had once been a bricklayer!

But that is another story. The miner's son responded by repaying his debts to this society with interest, both by from his presence and by his ideas which sprang experience and his essential gentle self. He wanted, as so many boys did, to play for Wales. He did so. He wanted to speak for and to Wales. In rugby football terms he did so. He also sought wider pastures, as a journalist, broadcaster, coach and critic, and he succeeded in all these spheres as well. In fact, he did almost everything he might ever have hoped to do, and if, at the end of his life there was a sense that he was still a man waiting for the nation to call him, and the nation did not, it was because he had expected too much.

In 1972 the councillor syndrome reappeared in his life, causing him a regret which he never fully balanced in his own mind. The greatest coach in the world never coached the Welsh team. It was a *cause célèbre*, one that he liked to encourage, especially abroad, but it was not quite as he sometimes made it seem, perhaps because for the first time in his life he had learned the pleasures of receiving the consolation of others. In a man so successful at everything, to fail was a unique experience.

Carwyn began his coaching career at Llandovery College where he assisted, then replaced T. P. Williams. Coaching at an adult level was practically unknown in the early 'sixties, but he had attended coaching courses run by the Central Council for Physical Recreation and later the Welsh Rugby Union at Aberystwyth University in company with other schoolmasters. He had built up a reputation as a schoolboy coach through the performance of his college side, and when the very first Welsh team coach, David Nash, was appointed by the Welsh Rugby Union in 1967, Carwyn's name was one of those considered. To put matters in perspective, however, the whole concept of coaching was then in its infancy and its pioneers were aware that there were sceptics and objectors even within the Welsh Rugby Union. When the appointment was made, David Nash was probably the most acceptable candidate to the union as a whole. He was an uncontroversial figure, free of association with any political party and was, in the words of John Taylor, a Welsh stalwart of the time, a quiet, shy man who immediately made his mark on the players. At that stage, it is likely that the fear of the principal advocates of coaching was simply that the whole concept would be dismissed, rather than objections made to a particular individual. It is also likely that Carwyn was not a strong contender and did not feel aggrieved when David Nash was selected. Carwyn had no experience of coaching senior teams in 1967, nor had most of his contemporaries, although he was appointed by the WRU committee to coach a West Wales XV against the 1967 All Blacks. Clive Rowlands, then at the end of his playing career, was his captain.

A year later, when Wales toured the Argentine, David Nash was not reappointed, even though he had laid the very first foundations of the most successful era for the Welsh rugby team. John Taylor, in *The Decade of the Dragon*, asserts that one of the reasons for David Nash's one-year term was that he 'was ill-equipped to deal with some of the political infighting', an opinion that lies like a voluptuous ruby upon the virginal innocence of most rugby books. Before the tour a new coach was to be appointed, and once more Carwyn's name was considered by the union, along with Clive Rowlands and

John Robins. The coach with the most experience of coaching adults was probably John Robins who had been with the Lions in 1966. However, Clive Rowlands, who had recently been elected as a member of the Welsh Rugby Union, was preferred. Rowlands, a dominant and flamboyant personality had the most recent playing experience, a factor which probably acted in his favour with the committee. He was also better known to them, very much an insider.

Once more Carwyn had been considered and turned down, but after the Argentinian tour, which was generally regarded as unsuccessful, the question of a new national team coach was raised once more, the appointment to coincide with a further Welsh tour of New Zealand in 1969. It was also decided that the coach appointed to accompany the team to New Zealand would be the Welsh National coach and when Carwyn was once again rejected and Clive Rowlands began his long tenure of office, insisting that he should be given a three-year term, he came to certain conclusions which were in the long run to add to his sense of grievance. There is no doubt that he felt bitterly disappointed and believed that he was not likely to be seriously considered unless he was a member of the WRU itself, that is, unless he achieved a political success in rugby terms and was present at meetings of all kinds. It was the natural desire of the man outside wanting to be inside. Accordingly, he stood for election as a district representative for his own district, but was again rebuffed. He was in con-tention with Hermas Evans, at the time a representative of Wales on the international board, and Myrddyn Jones of Loughor who had been elected only the previous year, and his decision to stand against them seems inexplicable. To unseat existing members in good standing would have been exceptional, and it is likely that Carwyn's decision to offer himself for election was no more than a token stance, in essence an announcement of his intention to stand in the future.

There are some who believe that he should not have

competed in a district election, but should have offered himself instead as a potential vice-president to all of the clubs in Wales, not with any immediate hope of success, but again as an indication of his future intentions, a common practice. In other words he, like everyone else, was expected to run for office and to follow conventional patterns of behaviour although, as in any duly elected body in South Wales, a nationalist would always be at a disadvantage.

Nationalists, including Carwyn, did not help their political cause when they pointed pious fingers at what they called 'one day Welshmen who wore their nationality on international match days only', or mispronounced the national anthem. There are always those (like myself) who do not necessarily see any special advantage in being Welsh *per se*. There is also your character to be considered, and the fact that badges of patriotism can be acquired easily enough. But Carwyn was a vigilante who had strayed into the badlands where the Welsh language and its shrinking territory was concerned, and he did not fully understand the aversion of those who felt themselves to be challenged.

Carwyn, at this time, it should be remembered, was also seen east of the pecos/Loughor River as a public schoolmaster, known to be outspoken and forthright, a likely rocker of the cosiest of boats, and even as a young pretender, an altogether different kind of man to those traditionally appointed to public office elsewhere. And it was not just public office. Some years later, when Clem Thomas suggested to John Samuel, Sports Editor of the *Guardian*, that Carwyn should write regularly on a contractual basis, thus reducing his own income as its Welsh Rugby Correspondent, the Cardiff Branch of the National Union of Journalists opposed Carwyn's necessary membership application and it was the Llanelli Branch who accepted him, since without it he could not work for a closed shop newspaper.

Prejudice, no less than coal, is a Welsh product that lies in seams but is never as difficult to mine. At around this time, I sat next to a Labour MP at a function and he offered me the definitive sentence on Aneurin Bevan. 'The trouble with Nye is that he spends too much time in the smoke-room of the House of Commons and not enough time in the bar with the other miners' MPs!' There was also, as noted in an anonymous portrait of Carwyn in the Welsh language magazine *Barn*, a quality from over the border to add to the conundrum. 'The fact is that there is something very English about Carwyn, his didactic and detached temperament; his emotional self-control, his refusal always to give freely of his thoughts, all contradict an intensely Welsh upbringing.' In short, he belonged but stood apart, perhaps because, in the words of one of his oldest friends, one time half-back partner and ultimately his BBC head of department, Onllwyn Brace, 'He lived and died by his own ability and would not tout for favours.'

Prejudice is a difficult thing to explain, but I can remember a sense of satisfaction in some quarters at Carwyn's defeat in the Welsh Rugby Union elections, more particularly when he stood for a vice-presidency in 1972. By this time, of course, he was much better known than he had been previously and had his Lions triumphs behind him. This sense of satisfaction at another's failure had its origins in the whole troubled history of Wales, because there is something about success which the disunited seem to resent. The very fact of it is a challenge, a threat to the joys of inertia, even a likely cause of interruption in the leisurely alternative art of interminable bickering. Nor is success a poultice to lay on the wounds of those who have never ventured. In some Welsh people (relatives of yours, not mine.) There is a Greek capacity for enjoying the woes of others, the salve of a victimised people who fear that the comfort of the crutch might cruelly be taken away when the White Blade strikes. 'And as for this fellow from where did you say it was? – well, as we all know, it was Clive's Lions players alone who beat the New Zealanders anyway, and in my day, the coach was something you passed out in!' (Begging your pardon, Councillor, but boys will be boys.)

Of course, it would be absurd to suppose that Carwyn in the role of White Blade, the terror of the Badlands, was the only Welsh thinker on the game of rugby football, or that there were no other coaches, or to ignore the fact that there were men who had fought hard for the very principle of coaching, estimable men all, or even that the Decade of the Dragon with its triple crowning glories would not have occurred without him. And while I am sure that not the slightest impropriety occurred, and the Welsh Rugby Union, democratic down to the last prospective committeeman managing to show his face in the bars of three rugby clubs per Saturday, demonstrating an acrobatic agility to capture the vote – all are blameless and free of any taint that is not widespread in the society which gave them birth – at the same time, there remains a sense of a talent unused, of a man unwanted who was somehow a man above his fellows and not of them, a man set apart by the very qualities of his intellect. (In his mind it should be noted, White Blade had never known the restrictions of the reservation as a lackey of any local authority and walked tall on the plains of employment, his only allegiance being to the Church in Wales, his ancient mentor in both Llandovery and Trinity Colleges.)

As for C. R. James, he well understood the ordinariness of ordinary people which is somehow compounded when they act in concert, clutching their rules and precedents, following their formbook like the slowest nags in the race. His mistake was that he said so. What he did not realise was that there were people who simply did not like him and saw him as a chapel goody-goody, a representative of a way of life that they had either never known, or were simply glad to be done with; but worst of all to them was his unclubbability, his aristocratic capacity for boredom. Neither the Head Prefect nor White Blade was in town to take more than the occasional dry sherry from the Warden, and as for skipping from one rugby club to another in search of votes, back-slapping was never on the itinerary. Custom and practice was for others. He might have

needed your spit-polished boots for Saturday's duty at the
Main Guard Gate, or would be very grateful if you could
manage to slice the top from a boiled egg 'Three minutes is
just about right!' – but where rugby football was concerned,
this very English Welshman was now learning to enunciate in
the 'I beg your pardon' tones that the Laird of Cefneithin
could take off to the manor born. There now appeared a long-
hidden capacity for not suffering fools gladly. He was also
not averse to talking openly to the press and indeed wrote
articles expressing his views with characteristic forthrightness,
itself unusual in Wales. That he was pressed to do so made no
difference. He also enjoyed it. Probably unknown to himself,
he was also being gently seduced by the media who at this
time pursued him like respectable streetwalkers, demure in
their bilingual black. At any rate, the streetwalkers came from
both sides of the street, smiling from all channels, and now
again he was tempted by an occasional television programme
and the odd journalistic piece. Fortunately, Wales has no Street
of Shame. It would be too expensive and, like the ancient
Kimmerian language itself (as described in Morien's *The History
of Pontypridd and the Rhondda Valley*), would need heavy sub-
sidy to survive.

But even if he had trailed his coat-tails and become talked
about, he was a rugby coach still, and from his point of view
he was successful. He had done everything he had been asked
to do, and his impact on the rugby world was immense. John
Taylor, a member of the successful Welsh and Lions's teams,
and now a journalist recalls,

> Few people had such a complete philosophy as to how
> the game should be played. He taught people that it
> wasn't just the bellowing shouting tub-thumper who
> could get things done. Such a coach wouldn't have got
> anywhere with the '71 Lions and it wasn't enough just to
> win because he saw the game as an art form, a great
> combination of the aesthetic and the competitive, which
> nothing else offered.

This concept of rugby as an aesthetic set pattern was to be the seed of his downfall. A thinker and a creative man, if there was one thing he knew, it was that committees could not create. Committees cannot paint pictures and when they write books they are only known as handbooks. The gold lettering embossed on the cover might be immaculate, and the little red book the only book read in the house, but it remains a handbook. In all Carwyn's experience, it was only by enforcing and persuading a single vision that the ultimate would be realised. It was the combination of the aesthetic and the competitive which drove him to want to express his own pattern, and to do that he needed lieutenants, not partners. Partners could keep the minutes. It was within this framework that he had succeeded in both New Zealand and Llanelli with Norman Gale playing the role which Ray McCloughlin began in New Zealand and Willie John McBride completed. In Llanelli, the triumphs occurred with a momentum of their own. In 1972, they reached the final of the WRU Cup Competition but lost to Neath, thereafter winning it for four consecutive years despite sometimes missing the services of key players away on tour. There were also further successes to come, although nothing quite equalled their victory over the 1972 All Blacks, 'a day', in the words of the WRU historians, 'for which they had waited for a hundred years!' They did not wait in vain.

The statistics, however, give only results not methods, and Carwyn's role comes alive only in the descriptions of those who knew him well. For Peter Rees, Llanelli's current president, he was 'a player's man and a treasurer's nightmare' for, displaying all the learned managerial arts he became the man who borrowed Manchester United's luxurious standards of treating players. 'He had no trouble with the Committee, but the Committee had trouble with him!' In Llanelli, he made his principal lieutenants Norman Gale and Delme Thomas, and his club backed him, accepting his priorities, allowing him to marshall the talents. They also left nothing to chance by appointing the services of a physical education expert, Tom Hudson, who produced 'the fittest and best prepared teams ever to emerge on to Stradey Park'. It was a fecund milieu in which the concept came to fruition, the single vision, the red coals of creation, the Scarlet triumphs! And 1972 was but the halfway mark.

At the time, both John Taylor and John Dawes felt along with many of their playing contemporaries that Carwyn was a natural successor to Clive Rowlands, but in 1972 Clive Rowlands had another two years to run as Welsh team coach and, it should be said, had a formidable record of success and few detractors. While Carwyn, in Dr Doug Smith's words, 'was keen to carry on for Wales, where he had left off in New Zealand', he must have felt that the official doors due to be opened in 1974 when Clive Rowlands retired, were likely to stick at the hinges, especially once his attempt to become a member of the union as vice-president had failed. Once more he was advised to stand again when there would be vacancies, but he never did. Instead, in 1974, perhaps knowing as a coach that time was running out, he declared war.

Writing to the Welsh Rugby Union in response to a circular letter, he replied as follows:

> Dear Sirs,
>
> Many thanks for the opportunity to allow one's name to go forward to be considered for the position of the Welsh National Team Coach.
>
> By implication only I gather that the terms of reference are as ever, that is, that the present system will continue.
>
> Am I to understand that the appointment is a three year one?
>
> Will the Big Five continue in its present form as a permanent institution?
>
> Will they be appointed annually – as at present – and the coach for three year periods?
>
> Since the present Big Five have already nominated

the coach of their choice, is it your honest assumption that any other nomination will be acceptable?

Will there be an interview for the post, and will the other applicants be told who is in contention?

I feel I have to ask all these questions, otherwise one is obviously compromising oneself totally. Any national team coach must surely have his own views on coaching, selection, team management etc., and these may not necessarily tie up with the present system. To be appointed, and then to disagree, leaves one in an invidious position.

The present Big Five obviously work happily together. They are a team, as they should be, and I respect them for it, and their nomination for the next coach suggests, rightly, that they want to remain as a team.

I personally feel that changes are now necessary. I will put my views very briefly because certain journalists, without reference to me, have 'jazzed up' a lengthy interview I gave to the Swansea *Evening Post* some time ago. These are my main points:

1. That the national team coach, as in some other countries, should always be the Chairman of Selectors.
2. That the Chairman of Selectors be allowed to choose two, three or even four advisers to help him – preferably three.
3. That preferably these would be coaches now active with their clubs.
4. That they would be chosen for their experience as players (forwards/backs) as coaches, and with reference to geography.
5. That the national team coach and his advisers should seek the assistance of all club coaches in Wales and attend club coaching sessions as from September. Wales, from a rugby point of view, is sufficiently small to put these ideas into practice. Elsewhere, they would be impracticable.

Wales has been at the forefront in its thinking in recent years. It is no use at the present moment for WRU members to bemoan the fact that other countries are catching up with us. The answer surely is that we must always try and out-think them.

Having considered my position over and over again, I have reluctantly come to the conclusion that I mustn't allow my name to go forward. I know that I'm asking too much of the Union – that change takes time. But I felt, however, that it was only fair to make my views known for the sake of the appointment – we all want the new man to be successful. He must be given the freedom to express himself.

A coach, like a teacher, is an expression of personality and he has to dominate if he is to succeed. This he can't possibly do with a small committee who were responsible for his appointment. Whatever the future policy, it is important, as a matter of principle, that he is appointed by the full executive committee of the union, and he should always be answerable to them. The dictator must observe humility!

My questions were rhetorical and I don't expect a reply.

Yours faithfully,
Carwyn James

It was, as no one can doubt, both the first and the last straw in his communications with the Welsh Rugby Union on the matter. With the letter and the newspaper interviews which preceded it, all laying down similar conditions, he had, as the *Auckland Star* proclaimed in far away New Zealand, cooked his own goose. He would not apply for the post – he would have to be asked, and then the other candidates would virtually have to be disrated.

And now he would never be asked. It was a disappointment that lay buried within him for the rest of his life. Merlin waited for the nation to call him, but the nation never did. Thereafter, he was, except for his two winter sojourns in Italy (which naturally ended in Rovigo winning the Italian championship), a rugby man on the sidelines, a journalist, a critic, an analyst, but still on the sidelines, a place he had no real wish to be.

Chapter Seven

Hunter and Hunted

'Come to Italy? Come on! You'll have a treat. You can work in the mornings. It's just like Llanelli, a small town. They're very friendly. We'll go to the opera.'

But when I wanted to go to the opera in Padua, there was difficulty getting tickets. He had lost interest.

'Stir yourself, James!'

But he didn't. I nagged again. I was doing the cooking and the washing-up. Even a fifteen-stone housewife wants to go out.

'What about Signor whatshisname – the President of the Rugby Union, or whatever? I'll bet he can get tickets!'

And, of course, he could. And did. We got to Padua by train, then a taxi through rain-washed streets. Carwyn was pre-occupied with his fly-half problem. He was going to relegate an international and promote a second fifteen player. The fathers of both players were ex-internationals, stalwarts of the club. They were opposing camps. It was his first controversial decision apart from imposing total silence on two or three teams of schoolboys who played on adjoining fields and gave off a cacophony of sound, their mouths opening and closing like penguins at feeding-time in a rugby zoo. But he got his way and they now played like overawed altar boys at an important funeral, giving new meaning to the New Zealand expression 'one-eyed'. Now they kept one eye squinting towards the touch line while he stood there, whistle in hand like a prep school tyrant. He could be that too. Even the schoolmaster referees seemed to move on tiptoe, becoming almost apologetic with their whistles. Now he was Signor Jam-es. When he blew for 'noise' even the referees froze.

We got to the opera house, late, out of breath and in a rush, diving into the auditorium. The house lights were down, the curtain was just about to go up when the manager appeared, puffing out his cheeks and wringing his hands to make an obviously important announcement. Raising his palm, he let forth a voluble burst of Italian which was immediately followed by a universal murmur of disappointment. Somebody was missing.

At first, Carwyn and I kidded each other about the amount of Italian we understood. He was preoccupied adjusting his seat, preparing to lose yet another raincoat. He raised his head alarmed.

'What's up?'

'Tough luck,' I said.

He looked around. The audience was fretful.

'*What?*'

'Delme Thomas has withdrawn,' I said. 'Cartilage trouble.'

When he laughed, it was with his whole face, a laugh which was sometimes accompanied by a giggle that would go on and on. He always liked the familiar joke and when abroad, he would see what was strange and identify it by means of the known parameters of home. He even catalogued the Italian players and journalists with the names or nicknames of those Welsh players or personalities whom they resembled in appearance. A joke would set him up for the evening and he had the capacity to become totally involved, especially in the theatre or in company when he was adept at persuading someone to talk. You could not be with him for long without realising that when he was not wholly engrossed in the task in hand, he relaxed completely, sagging and relying on his friends when he was not nodding off altogether. He once fell asleep on the pillion seat of a motorcycle which I was driving, a hazardous experience. This was a habit which was lifelong and indeed, retracing his footsteps after his death, I was to hear so many stories which were replicas of my own experience. Always a late night bird, even when he wasn't suffering from the virulent eczema which dogged him, he was a notorious daytime sleeper and catnapper. Once, as a young lecturer, he fell asleep during a tutorial, leaving a student sitting uncomfortably opposite him for nearly half an hour. The student was asked, 'Why didn't you leave him?'

'Well, I had one more question to ask him.'

That was Carwyn, always worth waiting for.

Since his death, re-travelling his journey through life, I have found that the facts, the places, matches won or lost, tell me nothing of the essence of the man. I knew him best when he was a journalist, occasionally sneaking off to advise teams like Cambridge University before the varsity match, but the man I knew was a different man to the intensely motivated figure in the tracksuit, the guru whom I just managed to glimpse in Italy. Once he gave up active and regular coaching in Wales, and once he realised that he was never going to coach the Welsh team, he entered another phase of his life, busy but less intent, more casual and at times almost purposeless, as if some of the steel inside him had eroded and nothing seemed quite so important any more. It made him more convivial, but under different pressures he became disorganised and so often more vulnerable. From the time he gave up lecturing to work freelance as a journalist, there were other subtle changes as he came to realise that he had to learn new disciplines, that it was not the minute but the second hand of the clock which mattered in the television studio.

I never discussed his famous letter to the Welsh Rugby Union with him, nor did I ever venture my opinion as to what might have been in his presence. Reading it now, I am forced to the conclusion that the Welsh Rugby Union could not have been expected to respond with open arms to such a letter and that the commonly held belief that Carwyn was mistreated by them in 1974 is erroneous. I did not then know the full circumstances, but some part of me divined his hurt. When others brought it up in company, he expressed not the slightest bitterness, simply changed the subject or withdrew. He said he was proud of the support he had received, but he was a man putting on a face when he said it. Now I am convinced he would have lived longer had he remained in the centre of things, for no sooner had he abandoned the safety of the institutionalised life with its set meals, ordered routines and not too demanding schedules, than he developed the eczema which became his cross.

However, it was the media which sought him, and he began his new career with a flourish. Leaving Trinity College, Carmarthen, in 1974, he did a series of television interviews for Harlech Television when he was seen in conversation with Neville Cardus, Willie John McBride and other famous sporting figures, including cricketers. They were programmes of instant appeal, but not least because he was himself a celebrity for whom other celebrities would make themselves immediately available and, as always, he took part in each interview as an enquiring equal rather than an interviewer proper, for conversation was his forte. He also broadcast frequently for the BBC and, by the time he became BBC Wales's rugby correspondent in 1974, he had written for the *Guardian* and also the *Western Mail* in which the 'Carwyn James At Large' column gave him the opportunity to cover a broad range of subjects. He must have had thoughts about journalism long before he became a freelance for he was already a spasmodic newspaper contributor and frequent broadcaster and, no doubt, even when he was lecturing saw an alternative way ahead. It was nevertheless an added complication in his dealings with rugby officialdom. Unlike the Warden of Llandovery College who was proud of his housemaster's broadcasting fame, an official body would have reservations, especially as some of his articles revealed his capacity for taking the occasional sideswipe at what displeased him.

In the *Western Mail* you would be as likely to find an exhortation to the Welsh team before a forthcoming international as a dissertation on the overpowering Anglo-American culture which was creating a rootless proletariat in urban Wales. He was against the raising of the school-leaving age to sixteen, against the comprehensive system, but defended the miners in the winter of discontent and quoted, with relish, Aneurin Bevan's attack on the British Medical Association, 'a small body of raucous-voiced, politically poisoned people!', an interesting group description that especially appealed to him. Then, at appropriate times, he would ask rhetorical questions. 'What would Saint David want of our lads on Saturday? That they keep their cool when the pressure is on, particularly in the early scrummages!' Saint David, very properly, was not invoked to advise the Welsh Rugby Union, although there was often a thrust at 'one-day Welshmen' or 'the breed who turned up in their dinner jackets on St David's Day at the Savoy', though he was later to enjoy such functions. When he was stuck with deadlines to make, he returned to pirate his unfinished autobiography and the readers of the *Western Mail* would suddenly find themselves sharing his childhood fantasies which were all the more intriguing when he turned to cricket.

> One of the great thrills to me as a boy was to watch Glamorgan play: a greater thrill even was to anticipate the game and play in it. I would always put the Aussies in first, feed them with lots of runs, take the occasional wicket, and then, moment of moments, HE would come in, the Great Man himself.
>
> How I used to hate him! I would attack his off peg, give the ball a lot of air and make it turn towards second and third slip, and I allowed him to thump the occasional one square and through the covers. But at the right psychological moment, I always got him with a straight quick low one and I appealed arrogantly and confidently – and he was out.
>
> *Bradman, D., l.b.w. James, C. 23.*

When he came to describe the West Indian cricketer, Everton Weekes, he surpassed himself:

> Before lunch he had scored 100 delightful runs, the like of which I have never seen before. It was cricket with art. The bat seemed to belong to his person, a part of the man's anatomy. A bit of wood, gracious, elegant, cultured, producing shots of such quality that one looked to the arts, to music and poetry, even to ballet to try to express them, such was his artistry.
>
> When he played back he seemed serious and contemplative and in the minor key; mostly he was joyously playing his symphony in the major, the sadness of his very being giving way to an optimism which lives only for that moment in the present when the skies are blue and warm, rare moments to be savoured there and then and for all time for they happen so seldom.
>
> It was impossible to bowl at him. That morning he made a mockery of the art of bowling. His front foot dominated and as it sprang to the pitch of the ball, in turn, cover, mid off and fielders straight behind the hapless bowler could only applaud as they acknowledged a passing acquaintance with the ball. This was genius born of accurate, rangy technique. Craft covered by inspiration, the romantic in a rare creative mood. I saw it and I shall never forget it.
>
> And then, in anger or in admiration, I shall never know, the heavens opened, it teemed torrential West Indian rain and Saint Helen's in no time at all was like a lake. Everything that day was done on the grand scale. It was not a day for mortals.

Carwyn was most successful as a journalist after he returned from Italy in 1977 when he now wrote a regular Friday column for the *Guardian*. He greatly admired Neville Cardus and to be associated with the *Guardian* gave him constant delight, as it did his readers. They would never know of his rage as when a sentence might be cut by a sub-editor, though he would sometimes telephone his friends to inform them! 'They messed it up! It was better than that. They don't understand!' His articles were seldom typed and more usually telephoned in, either by himself or his friends who would have the unenviable task of following the order of the paragraphs which might appear on separate pieces of paper, the backs of envelopes, or even the inside cover of the telephone directory, crossings-out as plentiful as phrases added vertically in the margin. There must be a legion of people, total strangers to journalism, who have nervously reversed charges and asked for the Sports Desk, beginning the tedious business of dictation and the painful spelling of obscure names to copy-takers bored with routine, ears growing numb while the author of the piece, abandoning his manuscript with total trust, was away enjoying himself. Having been a victim myself on many occasions, I once watched him one morning as he opened the *Guardian* to the sports page at the breakfast table and read himself approvingly. Then he gave his headmaster's solemn platform look and nodded gravely: 'You dictated that very well, I must say!'

What distinguished him when writing about rugby matters was his total authority, for he'd had a longer life in the game than most of his contemporaries. There was no one whom he could not approach and few who would not talk to him – he was ever a man to whom doors opened and his connections were worldwide, all assets to whoever employed him. His knowledge extended to other sports, particularly cricket, but it was rugby, of course, which took most of his time and readers of the *Western Mail* sports page on the week of a cup final in which Llanelli were playing would know exactly who smoked the last cigarette in the dressing-room, whose nerves played up most, and what it felt like to go down the tunnel on a big match day. Such information was later devoured avidly by the Italians when Carwyn became a columnist for one of their newspapers, and now and again he would fox them with quotations from Gwenallt, and also Milton's famous line: 'Who overcomes by force alone hath overcome but half his foe.' ('Was Signor James talking about forwards or backs?') Once, deputising for him when he had bronchitis, I covered a match in Aquilla, a rough, dirty game played with foul tempers on a soccer ground. Everyone was to blame, but at the end of the day a weariness took over and I concluded my piece by saying, 'As the sun went down, even the bad spirit waned, but for Aquilla, all the feathers flew in the wrong direction.' When translated and printed, it read, 'Aquilla played like men diseased.' 'This is the new journalism,' Carwyn explained, with poker face. He loved quoting R. C. Robertson-Glasgow who once ended a match report on a very boring game, 'Swansea played hard. The Barbarians played hard. None played harder than the Gwaun-cae-Gurwen Silver Band!' His column was eagerly awaited, the sports page the first to be read in the little local café's, and you would see the faces of old men wrinkle as they pondered his latest offering, no less fascinated than the young players. If he sometimes intrigued and puzzled them, or us, he was never boring, and now and again he would spot some young player of promise, maybe a twelve-year-old, and single him out for special attention. It was not the act but his authority which made it meaningful. No one who employed him ever got less than their money's worth, and he has never been replaced.

His greatest and most electrifying success was in television as a rugby analyst when he first appeared regularly in BBC Wales's *Sports-Line-Up*, a Sunday afternoon programme which featured the principal rugby match of the previous day and looked ahead to forthcoming encounters. He analysed games, discussed the Welsh team and drew attention to individual incidents, sometimes examining them closely with action replays so that you would see the blow that led to the blow that led to the referee's whistle. He was a firm believer in the use of television to clean up the game, and when he first appeared on a regular weekly basis, it was as if the general public had been let into the changing-room and you had a feeling that the Welsh selectors were bolting their Sunday luncheon in order to be perfectly composed for the occasion, pencil in hand. In its first years although he was sometimes accused of having scarlet (Llanelli) underwear and virtually exploded when Phil Bennett was dropped from the Welsh team – it was a programme that no rugby man could afford to miss. But it was a success that carried yet another peril for Carwyn soon became over-exposed and this led to further pressures. Having won his first international cap as a player, then a second as coach, he had now won a third television cap and became instantly recognisable, and accostable, to many more people and a genial prey for those who sought him. If he rode it all, it was only at a cost, because problems began even when the most minute household matters were neglected, matters for the most part which concerned himself alone, his diet, his appointments, his correspondence, even his laundry – when away from home, he was the most prolific buyer of shirts imaginable. He also broadcast frequently on radio discussion programmes, and since each separate broadcast requires that a contract be signed and returned by post to the broadcasting authority, with a carbon kept for income tax purposes, it is – you would have thought! – essential that these matters are dealt with promptly. But for a long period Carwyn neglected to sign the separate contracts and they piled up in his various bedrooms, briefcases or the back of his car with the result that BBC Wales had difficulty in balancing its books at the end of the financial year. He always had a number of other sources of journalistic income as well, and even in his Llandovery days, boys remember that he would occasionally have a clear-out and find cheques uncashed. He would look at them with amazement rather like an angler who has hooked some totally unexpected object. If they had expired, he would probably tear them up unconcerned, but if not, they would be sent in a bundle to the bank with a messenger. 'I wonder if you'd mind . . .' Matters reached a head when some thousands of

pounds worth of his BBC Wales contracts remained unsigned
and, indeed, he was employed as BBC Wales Rugby Correspondent, a job with a title and a monthly salary, at the
instigation of his friend Gareth Price, then Deputy Head of
Programmes, as much for the need to get administrative
matters straight as for his obvious desirability. It was the same
with invoices, bills, insurance, car tax or any such forms: they
came into his hands like leaves, only to blow away. When
questioned about some likely financial loss, he would say,
'It's only money.'

It was at this time in 1974 that Carwyn moved to Cardiff
where he stayed with his friend Derek Jones, a medical representative who became known as 'The Doc' and whose genial
hospitality was extended to visiting rugby celebrities, including
John Dawes on his periodic visits from London, with the result
that the roomy house in Penylan became known as the Coach
House. Had there been a visitors' book, its signatures would
have included half the world's rugby press, but it also contained those of cricketers like the West Indian Conrad Hunte,
the opera singer Delme Bryn-Jones, snooker commentators,
soccer managers like Dave Sexton, and visiting Italian players
short of a bed. Here, too, all the paraphernalia of the travelling
rugby life was to be found: tracksuits of many nations,
currencies of almost all, the rand mingling with the lire as
match programmes and fixture lists accumulated in a pile by
the telephone in the hallway. It was a telephone that was not
always answered with the precision the commercial world
expects, and was even on occasions disconnected, a Red Cross
procedure instituted to preserve the beauty of the early
morning which might otherwise be disturbed by persistent
editors wide awake in the southern hemisphere. If they did
make the connection, they would sometimes have to deal with
one of Mr James's involuntarily assembled staff. 'I don't care
if it is New South Wales – you'd have more chance if it was
Penygroes!'

It was from the Coach House that Carwyn, embedded in

his bachelor ways, began increasingly to travel across the world, moving from one sporting venue to another, eventually becoming careless with his diet and maintaining the marathon cigarette-smoking which he tried and failed to give up, with the result that it is difficult to think of him without calling to mind the wreaths of smoke, his early morning cough a prologue to each crowded day.

He seemed then to be a man always on the move, and yet he never ran, seldom even hurried, and was unconcerned about time, although off he went, here, there and everywhere, the cloud of smoke, the recently replaced raincoat, the battered suitcases, the crumpled match programmes, the latest rugby book clutched in his free hand as he disappeared into cars and airport lounges. Or sometimes he was to be seen on trains, composing one or other of his columns while in his wake, telephones rang and rang in the houses he had just left with a regularity that made householders flinch and enquirers increasingly ratty.

'It's the *Guardian*! It's *The Irish Times*! It's *Coal News*! It's *Round Table*! It's BBC Wales – Sport! Religious programmes, Vincent Kane on Friday, Monday, Tuesday, Wednesday, Controller, Head of Programmes, Assistant Head of Programmes – It's the Commissionaire's cousin Ifor from Pontyberem. My niece Blodwen is coming over from Australia with the two boys. One of them's named after Carwyn. I was wondering if there's any chance of a ticket . . .' 'I'm very sorry he's gone to Australia.' 'Oh, *darro*, missed him again.'

At other times, he was not where he was supposed to be, or late. It might be (and very frequently was) fog in Venice, or delays in Milan, and once, having hustled himself away to an expensive health clinic when he decided to slim, he was rescued by the Doc and driven at speed to cover a match in Ebbw Vale, stopping at the first Welsh valley fish and chip shop to indulge with a relief that was total. 'I shall not do that again!'

This is a composite picture of a lengthy period but it could be composed by any of Carwyn's friends. No sooner had he given up the ordered ways of the leisurely academic life than the skin infection which was to haunt him for the rest of his days began to manifest itself and, before long, it was sometimes painful to see him for although his face was unmarked, there were times when there was not another part of his body which was unaffected. Despite periodic treatment, including visits to hospital, it came and went like a sinister blush that later became infected, necessitating the regular application of ointments and creams which wearied him totally, until at last they replaced the forms and invoices as a measure of his indifference and went the same way, unlooked at and unused, except when those close to him nagged. The eczema and the scratching it caused, especially when his body temperature rose, induced a social embarrassment which he countered in the most stoic way. Carwyn dealt with his eczema by ignoring it, and in an extraordinary way his attitude passed on to his close friends for somehow it seemed quite natural for him to relax so totally that he was unembarrassed about removing his shoes and stockings, opening his shirt so that air could circulate and relieve the agony of those myriad tiny wounds. Oils, powders, creams, his habit of making another office in the bath where he sometimes lay for hours, made no difference, neither did sleep for he suffered and scratched constantly when the infection was at its worst. His attitude was at the same time both noble and tragic for he never complained, soon put you at your ease with a wry acceptance of his burden, and yet went manfully on with the way of life that entailed increasing amounts of foreign travel, hours and hours on aircraft as he crossed the globe, backwards and forwards, carrying off what to others would be a mortifying embarrassment with an insouciance that was complete. It is a terrible thing to describe – if an animal had suffered so, you would have destroyed it without compunction – and yet this condition, sometimes half-controlled, sometimes not, represented for me the source of

Carwyn's vulnerability and his immense courage. It was an heroic stoicism you would not have expected, as intractable as his mother's asthma had been, but he went his way unabashed for as long as he could, finally collecting doctors and medical specialists as intimates for his entourage, but, within himself, without any real hope of permanent cure. He could not change his erratic and frenetic way of life and although he made sporadic attempts they did not endure. The tragedy was that the immaculate man, the fly-half who side-stepped so elegantly on shadows slowly became a sick man who was never to sit in reflective comfort in his old age, nor indeed to have the time or the inclination for the joys of marriage or parenthood although he had several intensely loyal women friends on whom he could and did call when he was in need of comfort and support, and – literally – when his wounds needed dressing.

At the same time he seemed to prefer houses where there were children, for he was at home in the family atmosphere. Yet there was on my part a certain amount of envy or jealousy: like all his married friends, I knew how he could and did expose us fathers for the irritable beings we sometimes are. With children or young people who perhaps have a special way of knowing who is genuinely interested in them and who is not, Carwyn always had the time. He was never too tired when there was a cricket bat lying idle, and there are half-a-dozen or so families spread across the United Kingdom with whom he often stayed where he was the complete dustbin cricketer, often taking up a tennis ball on cabbage patch pitches outside where he would bowl leg breaks by the hour, turning a ball effortlessly to the delight of all the neighbourhood children who would somehow know that he had arrived. He played every game you could think of, was a tactician in all, and would send blue balls buzzing on miniature plywood snooker tables perched on the sofa as easily as he did when all eyes were upon him in a crowded billiard room, especially late at night when all good people have gone to bed. This was the man who at eleven had been selected by the committee to play snooker in the welfare hall against Sidney Smith, at that time in the same league as Fred Davies and Walter Lindrum. He was ever the man for the big occasion, but never forgot what it was like to be eleven. Once, opening the door to a young friend of my son's who stared at the famous face for some time without quite recognising it, he was greeted by a solemn enquiry. 'Mister, are you the coacher?'

He nodded gravely. It shall be his epitaph.

But not yet.

In Italy, he was to have another familiar disappointment after his team won the Italian championship, at which he was photographed with the Pope – a portrait that was to be published around the world and was once captioned, 'Who is that with Carwyn James?' He had hoped to be national coach to the Italian team, but the French full-back, Pierre Villepreux, was chosen, and Carwyn returned to Wales to resume his old role as BBC Wales's rugby correspondent and to intensify the journalistic life he had led before. By this time, he was also a director of a Cardiff travel firm, a connection which was to secure him the air tickets which allowed him, at short notice, to cross the world at will, and there now began a period of his life when he seemed to be rugby football's Mister Everywhere. As well as his regular Friday piece for the *Guardian*, he did a year's stint giving a match report or an opinion for the *Sunday Mirror*, and contributed at various other times for newspapers as diverse as the *Glamorgan Gazette* and *The Scotsman*. He also wrote for Welsh and Italian language newspapers, *Welsh Rugby Magazine*, and a host of others. You had but to ask him, and he provided, although it was his *Guardian* column which pleased him the most and over which he took the most care. He appeared less frequently on television, but was always to be seen before or after an international match, and his opinion was the most sought on any controversial issue. He became a regular radio broadcaster, giving opinions or summaries, and occasionally commentated in Welsh. In the summer of 1977, he led a party of tourists to follow Phil Bennett's Lions team across New Zealand, combining the unlikely role of courier with journalist as he sent match reports home on radio. Soon after that he became involved with a major BBC Wales TV series, *The World of Rugby*, which examined the history of the game and its development throughout the world. A collaboration with John Reason of *The Sunday Telegraph* resulted in a companion volume published by the BBC, although the programme itself was to be the indirect cause of one of the few instances when he was criticised by the Welsh language press.

In 1969, Carwyn had coached the Llanelli team against the South African touring side, although he expressed his hatred of apartheid by refusing to watch the match. But in 1978, during the filming of *The World of Rugby* TV series, while Cliff Morgan, a co-presenter, went to the Argentine, and Dewi Griffiths, the producer, went to New Zealand, Carwyn flew to South Africa where he met Dr Danie Craven, the President of the South African Rugby Board, a leading thinker on the game. They stood together on the terrace at Newlands in Cape Town to watch the first ever match between white and coloured sides. Carwyn seems to have given no thought to the possibility that such a game might be no more than a cosmetic exercise which would make no substantial change to the position of black rugby players, particularly schoolboys, although his view of apartheid remained unchanged. It was much too exciting an occasion – as far as rugby football was concerned, a meeting of giants – and Carwyn made another friend. He also enjoyed meeting the South African centre, Johnny Gainsford, whose book, *Nice Guys Come Second* was, as you might expect, about rugby tactics, with no moral intended off the rugby field, unlike Carwyn's own pronouncement on the platform of the National Eisteddfod, 'They tell me the best way to defend is to attack!' The sheer delight at the completion of his rugby education amongst those who shared the greatest passion of his life was simply too great for Carwyn's political beliefs, and this visit was the first of many to South Africa. Once, after accompanying Clem Thomas and John Reason to cover the 1980 Lions's tour, he ended his final report with a glowing compliment both to his two friends and to the rugby environment. Asked how he had enjoyed the tour, he replied, 'I wish it could have gone on for ever!'

But the code was broken as far as his political friends were concerned. He had transgressed the absolute stand demanded by opponents of apartheid and he was taken to task in a Welsh language newspaper. Later, the Welsh Council of Churches wrote to him to express their disfavour. Those of convinced views did not find it hard to criticise him, and some believed that the very act of changing his mind indicated a diminution of his mental processes. My own view is that he simply could not keep away. There was a touch of Richmal Compton's *Just William* in Carwyn which revealed itself even on a political platform as his notes for his election speeches indicate, one pencilled thought posing the question and answer, 'What sort of industry do we need? – Best of all, no industry at all!' His visits to South Africa were a case of rugby football being at one with Lady Nicotine. He could give up neither even if the world were in flames and, indeed, on one visit to hospital when his skin condition had become unbearable, he gravely asked a friend to stop the car and despatched him to purchase five hundred non-tipped cigarettes which he could smuggle in, hopefully to last the week. As for the diminution of his mental processes, I was with him when he received the protesting letter from the Welsh Council of Churches. He thought it an impertinence, completed his morning cough and grunted sardonically.

'Bloody cheek!' he said. 'I've got a cousin on that too!' It was, and continued to be, a fall from grace, but I still could not but wish him the pleasure of the company he sought. The Cefneithin honours went instead to Barry John whose book made direct statements:

One day we were taken to see gold mines and, of course, there were many black men working there. We saw a group of them loaded into a cattle truck – they weren't treated like human beings at all.*

After Italy, Carwyn's gypsyish rugby life began anew. If he was like a man on a moving staircase moving inexorably to its final destination, it was the life he had chosen and it was not until his first collapse in 1982 that the pressures of it seemed quite so obvious as they do in retrospect. The truth was, he lived a divided life, sharing himself out amongst his friends and family, and was so often on the move that you would seldom see him for long periods. When you did, it was like the immediate resumption of all the old good times, now to be encapsulated in whatever time he could spare, or rather whatever time his professional life allowed him since there were weeks when he had so many appointments and had to be in so many places that it was as if he was being ruled by a diary compiled by someone else, some omnivorous and many tentacled monster that lived at the end of all those telephones.

'Hello, Carwyn!' we said, knowing at that instant that there was hardly ever a time with him that was unenjoyable. He might be an hour or a day late, you didn't care, and this is the hardest thing to describe for the private man was as enchanting with his few faults as the public man should have been formidable with his many achievements – but he was not. He was a legend to all those who did not really know him, but at the same time a mystery to those who did, for there was something about him which came alive only in response to certain stimuli and for a great deal of the time he was a man of silences, with a marked aloofness when it pleased him. And yet, in recall, he is never aloof, perhaps because the memory selects and the times you remember best are so crowded with incident that in the end it is your own pleasure which you are remembering because if ever a man cast a light it was him. He

* *The Barry John Story*, Collins, 1974.

had, in Max Boyce's lovely phrase, 'a key to another door of a house I'd lived in all my life', which is to say that he was a man who enlarged a moment for his friends and immediately brightened the day, especially when he arrived suddenly and unexpectedly, to take up where he had left off before.

He was such an expert at dismissing the past and preserved few animosities, although when I laboured long and hard for twelve months in 1979 researching the Welsh Rugby Union's Centenary Film, *A Touch of Glory*, and decided to publish a short literary essay on the history of the game 'to include the memoirs and imaginings of a fan', and received not a word of thanks but an official letter from the WRU gravely informing me of the committee's displeasure at my having chosen to write a book, not an unusual activity in the life of a professional author – Carwyn's laughter filled the house. It was as if the collective ignorance and stupidity lay buried like some subterranean substance beneath the impassive faces of seemingly normal men, by day shopkeepers, schoolmasters, commercial travellers, policemen and the like, to emerge vaporised once they donned their little brass insignias of rank, like some stupifying nerve gas whose emission was exclusively reserved for dealings with those outside the group. The film was official and recorded in the minutes so that was allowable, but because I had written a book I was violently accused by one worthy of 'making money off the backs of young players', as if, like the hard-faced men who make profits out of war, I was in some way suddenly in the munitions business while the flower of Welsh youth were being decimated below the luxurious free-drink suite in the new National Stadium. Three thousand copies of my short essay equalled three thousand bullets.

'Next time you meet them, take a cigar!' Carwyn said, and indeed, he gave me a box by courtesy of Rothmans for whom he often appeared in rugby 'Brains Trusts' throughout Wales.

On another occasion in one rugby club, I was pushed bodily against a lavatory wall and held forcibly by the chest. What had I done now?

'There's too —— much about —— Newport in that —— film, you silly ——!' my assailant said, using a variety of vehement adjectives.

You would like to reply that the collective sexual accomplishments of Newport Rugby Football Club over the years, beginning with the Prince of Welsh threequarters, Arthur Gould (who bears a striking resemblance to Omar Sharif), were probably none the less remarkable or unremarkable than say, Ystradgynlais or Bedwas RFC. But in the circumstances, hard up against the white tiles, the inflamed and bloodshot eyes bearing down upon you, the dilated nostrils, the saliva bubbling on parted lips, three of four brownish teeth visible – the apoplectic whole held threateningly only inches away (the dimly-lit lavatory is also empty apart from your assailant who has followed you in there) – what do you do? 'Sorry,' I said. Shelley's fading coals of creation have long interested me, perhaps because I fade so badly. 'Very sorry, Newport are having a bad season, I'm glad to say.'

Carwyn, of course, enjoyed all this immensely, and when he suggested I write a short piece for the *Guardian* on the subject of the Welsh centenary, he mischievously told people, 'He is making thousands! "The Onedin Line" is chicken-feed compared to it!' It was as if, in my brief encounter with Welsh rugby officialdom, a new experience for me, I was suddenly being drawn by him into the closed world which, alas, he had provided with a very good excuse for rejecting him. But he never spoke about it although my own experiences gave him the pleasures of a continuing comic strip. Just as he had run home early from school to follow the adventures of Rupert the Bear in the *Daily Express* so my progress was daily monitored, and when I discovered that the James Brothers, one of the most famous and impish half-back partnerships in Welsh rugby history, were half-Jewish, his delight was total. 'That's a piece for the *Jewish Chronicle*!' And indeed, prompted or unprompted, the *Chronicle* later telephoned me. I did not know then that Carwyn and Onllwyn Brace playing as youngsters for Llanelli

mischievously interchanged positions at half-back, exactly as
the James Brothers had done, throwing the ball between their
legs, here, there and everywhere, during a rout of Plymouth
Albion, but were grimly told by their captain R. H. Williams,
now a Welsh selector, 'We don't want any of that Harlem
Globetrotters stuff against Neath!'

Carwyn enjoyed his friends as much as they enjoyed him.
What was crucial was his lack of interest in himself, and his
total concern for you. In this respect, he was like a mirror, old
fashioned and a little chipped at the edges, but nevertheless a
mirror from which you came away with a better reflection of
yourself. It is an inadequate metaphor, but it describes the
golden aspects of his character, his genuineness and the never
faltering concern for his intimates. You could disagree with him,
grow impatient with him, be occasionally exasperated at some
minor intransigence or other, but the residue remained, his
essential gentleness. He was, as the young student noted,
always worth waiting for.

He also had the knack of distracting all attention from
himself, and when his friends and family grew concerned
about him, and his skin condition in particular, if he could not
divert your attention he would vanish. Carwyn James was a
boring topic to Carwyn James unlike your latest novel, your
new song, your last programme, the remark made by so-and-
so to so-and-so or, better still, the recent intelligence about the
Welsh Rugby Union, which he sometimes called 'the Onion'.
'Did you know they actually took the Welsh team to see *Babes in
the Wood* before the Twickenham match? They couldn't get
into the Black and White Minstrels, so, with four years to book
up, that's what they come up with. Can you imagine the
Pontypool Front Row watching *Babes in the Wood*?'

And he, and you, would be off. He did not want to bore you,
or himself, with the afflictions of Carwyn James. It was the
same with all his friends, his family who cared for him dearly,
for he was all his life a cherished man. Carwyn the friend was
a unique and beloved man of greater consequence than all his

public achievements, and the reason why he taxed so many of his obituarists, many of them journalists who found themselves stunned at the news of his death, sitting silently beside the telephone while they struggled to find the right phrase. To Clem Thomas, 'He was not a saint, but he had saintly qualities', while Cliff Morgan remembered what had been said about George Gershwin. 'I know he's dead, but I don't have to believe it if I don't want to.' For Colin Welland, 'When I heard he was dead, I felt as if a branch line of my life had been cut off. He was an excursion I could take, a different path in the game of creation. Now it's finished.' For Professor Dafydd Bowen, 'When he died, I felt a part of me died also, although I hadn't seen him for years, but I felt he was always there on tap.'

It was an experience felt by many, for the gift of himself was the most precious to all who had the good fortune to know him well. In my own case, he has left me a deadly legacy since he loved language and treasured remarks, the asides of the famous and the infamous, and there was a game we played on damp nights after training sessions when the restaurant keepers meaningfully put up their shutters and he simply would not go to bed. It was a game of sentences, the most cutting you could compose; sentences for the most boring of occasions, at first for general use, later for people you knew, or better still had not yet met, but might do.

I have already related the template, 'There is something in what you say, and no doubt you have your contribution to make, however small.'

Then, for use on enforced official occasions (a real votegetter): 'Well, it's been a pleasure! I must say, it's a great change for me to mix with such extremely ordinary people as yourselves! Very interesting indeed.'

This went on until finally we began to consider people he knew including those in high office, to whom Carwyn would introduce me, at some time in the future, my dialogue already succinctly composed.

'Director General, did you say? How d'you do? James tells me I might have had you under me in the Service!'

If the dialogue composed was all uttered in the accents of the long-forgotten monocled naval captain whom Carwyn used to imitate with a tablespoon to his eye, it was a tendril from the past. The truth was, he was usually the most circumspect of men, born to grace school Speech Days and Eisteddfod platforms, the soul of propriety who would never offend anyone, but he retained the imp of mischief which was equally a part of him and without which no portrait would be complete. And now sitting here, one half of the biting team is finally bit, for the boot is on the other foot and I can hear his voice and see his pen in a similar game, the minute handwriting sloping up the side of whatever scrap of paper is to hand. He would play the game on me with the greatest relish – and fun.

'Mr Richards, having little knowledge of the Welsh language and less of the Welsh countryside, has taken it upon himself to attempt a biographical essay on a notable Welsh figure. He would have been better advised to marshal his few thoughts towards Turkestan where authorship is not normally confused with ventriloquism.'

It is a game you can play all night.

'Mr Richards, once aptly described as a rugby-forward "slow but dirty", has brought the often hoarsely expressed views of the terrace and the tanner bank into tactical discussions of rugby football at the highest level. The most accurate comment that can be made is that he writes like a Welsh selector. Some inherit the wind, some create it: he is it.'

And so on.

Carwyn was all the things I have said he was, Carwyn the Blameless, Head Prefect, 'Just William', Merlin, The Laird of Cefneithin, White Blade and Federal Marshal, hunter and hunted and the scourge of the plains of mediocrity, the over-weight elitist and restaurateur's delight who, escaping from a health clinic – 'You couldn't even get a bet on a horse there!', drove on in grim silence until he could not move a foot further without his Welsh fish and chips! As a child he was privileged, thanks to the love and thrift of his parents and family who did not have to face the brutal realities of the eastern coalfield where others were driven to violence, despair and penury, and, of course, in spite of but as a result of all their struggles, to provide a substantial number of the leaders who were the instruments of political and social change in the United Kingdom as a whole. Carwyn was unimpressed by this, being old-fashioned in the modern sense, protected by rural hearts in an industrial enclave. His political stance was cultural, and nothing indicates it more than his election speeches, the one note in red ink amongst his papers a clear indication of where his heart lay, a quotation from the Welsh radical, Henry Richard of Tregaron:

> The people who speak this language (*i.e. Welsh* – Carwyn's italics, not mine!), who read this literature, who own this history, who inherit these traditions, who venerate these names, who created and sustained these marvellous religious organisations, the people forming three-fourths of the people of Wales – have they not a right to say to this small propertied class . . . 'We are the Welsh people and not you?' 'This country is ours, not yours, and we claim to have our principles and senti- ments and feelings represented in the Houses of Parliament!'

How we would all have cheered – in 1868, when these thoughts were first uttered to the newly enfranchised and then largely Welsh-speaking electorate of Merthyr Tydfil. But Carwyn, like his party, never really came to terms politically with the rest of us, those who see no road back to that homogeneous society and will have to fashion the future out of the Wales and the Welsh people who now exist, irrespective of their antecedents, and ever mindful of their rights to speak whatever language they choose, free of stigma and without restriction in the employment they seek.

Perhaps Carwyn never gave sufficient weight to the early life of his favourite writer, Gwenallt, who wrote with such passion:

> Capitalism was something living to us. We saw the poverty, famine and near famine, the hovel-like houses, mothers growing old before their time, the cruelty of soldiers and policemen during the strikes, doctors putting tuberculosis instead of silicosis on the death certificate to avoid the paying of compensation to relatives, and the bodies coming home after accidents. Years later, my father's body came home after he had been burnt to death by molten metal, and that unnecessarily. When in the funeral sermon, the minister said that it was God's will, I cursed his sermon and his God with all the haulier's swear words I knew, and when they sang the hymns at the graveside, I sang in my heart the *Red Flag*.*

Gwenallt was to reject Marxism as he had once rejected Christianity, and returned to the fold, becoming a nationalist, suspecting the power of workers' leaders who 'betrayed the workers on strike'.

In a gentler time, Carwyn had no such conversions in his life, but for all that, he was a product of the Welsh hearth and never forgot his loyalties, always standing up for the place and the people who formed him, and yet moving subtly beyond it and them. He was a hero in all his worlds, a classic outside-half and a chapel deacon, a journalist and the manipulator of journalists who once, seeking to distract the attention of the press from the injuries of one of his famous players in New Zealand, began his daily press conference with the bogus announcement of his engagement to a fictional air hostess 'That'll keep 'em guessing!' – the same man who could not refuse the *Llanelli Star* or the *Glamorgan Gazette* a quick article or opinion even if he'd had but a few hours of sleep in a week.

---

* transl. Andre Morgan and Ned Thomas, *'Credaf'*, *Planet* 32.

As a political candidate, he was a university lecturer, as a rugby coach – 'the bard of coaches' – he learned eagerly from everyone, most of all from his lifetime's experience and delight. As a teacher he was always a conversationalist, and as a friend he was incomparable. Only as an invalid was he a disaster for he was simply not interested in looking after himself. Chided for never having written the book he always promised, he finally put together a coaching manual, *Focus on Rugby*, published posthumously, which will stay in print for a decade since it is a part of his credo, an attack on regimentation and a plea for the mastery of basic skills which will long outlive his most misquoted statement, 'Get your retaliation in first', a simple and innocent instruction relating to group movement across the lineout, the law-maker's nightmare. Its last chapter missed deadline after deadline and was finally taken by hand to London, a desperate journey to the waiting publisher. The hand was Max Boyce's who was travelling by special coach with a group of BBC dignitaries to attend a service held in St Paul's Cathedral to commemorate the seventy-fifth anniversary of the BBC in the presence of the Queen. When he got there, he found his way blocked by the police who would not let him penetrate a cordon to rendezvous with the waiting publisher's representative.

'Don't you understand? I've got the last chapter of Carwyn James's coaching manual?'

They did not. Ten thousand people waiting to see the Queen and the rendezvous impossible, the last chapter finally found its way by another courier's hand, the opera singer Stuart Burrows who got it to the Savoy Hotel where it was snatched for the printing presses that very afternoon. It was a drama that well pleased its author, a near hiatus that nevertheless ended in another task brilliantly completed. For the final version of the book represents a fitting last testament to his rugby beliefs, the coacher's last word with, as usual, grateful thanks due to all his lieutenants along the way.

As for the man, he would not wish any sad songs to be sung

for him. He succeeded in almost every phase of his life and if I have related my disagreements with him, it is because, fundamentally, they did not affect our friendship, for more than anything, he was a very human, human being.

I missed his last telephone call asking me to come with him to Amsterdam. My daughter took it instead. He had been working continuously on a rugby television series which, as usual, resulted in a good deal of travel – to Paris to see Jean-Pierre Rives, to Ireland and Scotland and elsewhere and he was exhausted. I wanted him to take a winter break in the sun, to the Canary Islands where, as I always urged, he could take his shirt off and feel the sun on his back, that poor lacerated skin.

'Why don't you come?'

I couldn't spare the time.

'Come on!'

I hesitated. It had been an age since I received a letter from the Italian rugby authorities, enclosing an air ticket asking me to travel with the London Scottish! Carwyn fixed that with a smile. Now he was insistent.

'Come on! We can fish.'

I'd introduced him to mackerel fishing the previous summer. He'd dropped a fish fag with twelve hooks over the side of the boat. Twelve fish came up. We'd hit a shoal. He expected it as of right. Quite normal. 'Every-egg-a-bird, James!' I said.

But I couldn't manage yet another holiday. He couldn't get a flight to Lanzarote from Cardiff. He gave the travel agent only three days' notice! Instead, he went to Amsterdam, the first flight available to anywhere. 'Where will I stay?' Somebody told him there was a five-star hotel where Hitler had once stayed. 'That'll do!'

In Amsterdam on 8 January 1983, he collapsed of a heart attack while shaving, striking his head against the bath, and died. He was not found for some time and one enquirer was told that he had checked out of the hotel, a confusion that would have amused him. In his last telephone call home the previous night, his first question had been to enquire of Llanelli's result in the Welsh Cup tournament. He was disappointed. Shortly before, he had expressed his disapproval of my daughter's change of boyfriend, despite the fact that the replacement was Welsh-speaking. They were quintessential Carwyn telephone calls, the usual checking up on those he cared about.

It was fitting that he should have had three memorial services, in Welsh, English and Italian, where all the people from all his worlds seemed to assemble. His death commanded more obituary space than that of a cabinet minister. The newspapers proclaimed it in banner headlines, PRINCE OF COACHES DIES, WALES STUNNED BY COACHING MAESTRO'S DEATH. Representatives of the Welsh Rugby Union mingled with their English counterparts, media men and women, his huge family of friends, all finally united in tribute as he would have wanted it, being essentially a man without personal animosity. At a Swansea v. Llanelli match, there were the customary tributes, the secretary asking for a moment of silence to mark the passing of Carwyn James, 'Rugby man, scholar and patriot'.

If the silence was like a groan for we knew that we would not see his like again, now we have had time to reflect. He was fifty-three when he died; of himself when eight-years-old, he had written:

> Dafydd Morris next door, with whom I go to prayer meetings in Tabernacle, kneels and his mind gropes for his favourite Godly idioms, slowly, falteringly, seeking delay from the occasional lengthy neighing cough. I feel nervous and want to help him as phrase leads to phrase for I have heard them all so many times before. With my left hand over my face, I open two fingers slightly enough to peer at the slow moving finger on his large face of the clock made in Birmingham – and note with relief, as Dafydd hits second gear, that ten minutes have gone.

Another five and a whole torrent of bits of hymns and scripture, but coughless and unpunctuated, will pour forth in a mad overdrive crescendo, and as he ends I shall wipe the sweat from my brow. I like Dafydd Morris, and I practise his Wednesday prayer on my own in private. Tonight in the chapel vestry, the going is hard; the sun is still hot outside, and above the buzzing of the claustrophobic bees I can hear the thud of ball on bat, of bat on ball, and the occasional recognisable soprano appeal. As in turn Thomas Evans kneels, I wonder if I shall have a knock before going home.

My own reflection is a happy one – he certainly had his knock. He would have liked the metaphor. Like Neville Cardus, he had his good innings and played all the strokes he knew, many of them elegant and stylish, the touch of class he so admired, the essential difference. Now he is free of pain, yet very much alive and sparkling in the memory of the privileged ones who knew him – a glass in hand, for he was the most convivial of men, a cigarette going, the ash falling on the page as he looks over your shoulder.

'Don't know how to end, eh? Strike a bold note!'

'Very well. Here goes . . .

His end, like the game he loved, was heavily sponsored.

'Fags, you mean? Untipped, you mean? Oh, well, I've had a good life. I have no regrets.'

Let no one doubt that the President of Llanelli Rugby Football Club was well capable of writing his own epitaph, and just did.

What also needs to be said is that he was a Welshman who made you feel glad you were a member of the human race.

Index